Better PowerPoint®

D1009089

STEPHEN M. KOSSLYN

Better PowerPoint®

Quick Fixes Based on How Your Audience Thinks

OXFORD
UNIVERSITY PRESS

OXFORD
UNIVERSITY PRESS

Oxford University Press, Inc., publishes works that further
Oxford University's objective of excellence
in research, scholarship, and education.

Oxford   New York
Auckland   Cape Town   Dar es Salaam   Hong Kong   Karachi
Kuala Lumpur   Madrid   Melbourne   Mexico City   Nairobi
New Delhi   Shanghai   Taipei   Toronto

With offices in
Argentina   Austria   Brazil   Chile   Czech Republic   France   Greece
Guatemala   Hungary   Italy   Japan   Poland   Portugal   Singapore
South Korea   Switzerland   Thailand   Turkey   Ukraine   Vietnam

Copyright © 2011 by Stephen M. Kosslyn

Published by Oxford University Press, Inc.
198 Madison Avenue, New York, New York 10016

www.oup.com

Oxford is a registered trademark of Oxford University Press

Library of Congress Cataloging-in-Publication Data

Kosslyn, Stephen Michael, 1948–
Better PowerPoint : quick fixes based on how your audience thinks / Stephen M. Kosslyn.
p.   cm.
Includes index.
ISBN 978-0-19-537675-3
1. Business presentations—Graphic methods—Computer programs.
2. Microsoft PowerPoint (Computer file)   3. Presentation graphics software.   I. Title.
HF5718.22.K67 2010
658.4'520285558—dc22

                                                          2009030696

9   8   7   6   5   4   3   2   1

Printed in the United States of America
on acid-free paper

Preface

Presentations: We've all sat through them, wondering why we're there; or we've given them, wondering whether the audience cares. This is a book about how to make presentations effective and therefore more interesting to the audience members.

Years ago, I was at a conference where one of the most distinguished cognitive scientists in the world, an expert in how the mind processes information, was wandering though a PowerPoint® presentation and losing the audience in the process. I thought about the number of presentations I had heard where the presenters did not accommodate their audience members' short attention spans, difficulty reading small type, need for organization, and other strengths and weaknesses. As a scientist, I started thinking about how to use well-known laboratory findings to improve presentations. And then I wrote a book.

My book *Clear and to the Point* addressed all aspects of presentations and discussed eight "rules" about how our minds work: the same eight rules discussed in this guide. In that book, I assumed that the reader was starting from scratch and would read the book cover to cover. Although generally well received, it soon became clear to me that there is still a need for another, more focused book—for at least two reasons: First, most people interested in PowerPoint® presentations have already made at least one presentation; they are not PowerPoint® innocents. Second, people who want a book on presentations want one that they can use easily, not one they can take to an evening chair and read cover to cover.

With these considerations in mind, this book distills the core of my earlier book into a quick guide on how you can revise a presentation you already have in hand. I have also added new material, partly in response to feedback I received regarding the earlier book. This book is organized so that you can easily revise your presentation in a couple of hours, using checklists at the start of each chapter to help you improve your work.

Does the world really need yet another book on electronic slideshow presentations? Since my previous effort, a number of superb books on this topic have been published. Garr Reynold's *Presentation Zen* and Nancy Duarte's *slide:ology* immediately spring to mind as outstanding contributions. The available books, however, assume that readers are starting from scratch, much as I did, and also assume that readers have plenty of time to perfect their work. In fact, it's easy to defend the recommendation that you should spend 30 to 90 hours to prepare a slideshow and craft your presentation. But I have long lived with the realities of being on the road, with having to prepare and revise presentations on the fly. In my experience, we keep having ideas about how to tune our presentations right up to the point where we have to deliver them. Moreover, most of us don't have art departments to assemble slides for us, as some of the other books sometimes seem to assume. This book is written as a practical guide for today's road warrior who needs to tune up an existing presentation, and do so quickly.

I have many people to thank for inspiring and helping me make this book a reality. First, Laurence Alexander suggested that I write this book, and provided useful advice at every turn. Second, Catharine Carlin of Oxford University Press once again proved invaluable (this is the fourth book I have done with her); Catharine once again saved me from myself. Third, Alexandra Russell and Jennifer Shephard gave me useful feedback on an earlier draft (and Alex, Jennifer, and Rogier Kievit collaborated in the studies that I summarize briefly in Chapter 1 and in the Epilogue, which are reported in Kosslyn, S. M., Kievit, R. A., Russell, A. G., and Shephard, J. M. [2009], *PowerPoint® presentation flaws and failures: A psychological analysis.* Submitted for publication). Dan Willingham provided valuable advice about how to present this material, which was much appreciated. Fourth, my agent Rafe Sagalyn once again proved to be a creative problem solver. Next, I need to thank everyone who contributed to *Clear and to the Point* (noted in the preface to that book)—I built on their wisdom, and have lasting gratitude for their time and trouble. Finally, I must thank my family, once again: Robin, who forgave me for being (slightly) late in finishing portions of our jointly authored textbooks, and our children, Justin, David, and Neil, who proved that there is no substitute for being immersed in technology from an early age.

Contents

Better PowerPoint®

Chapter 1

The No-Stress Approach

PowerPoint Jedi use their skills at PowerPoint to make difficult concepts clear. Me, I'm a PowerPoint Sith. I use my PowerPoint skills to confuse and obfuscate. If my boss doesn't have a glazed look of bewilderment, then the brief isn't complete. Embrace the dark side.

—MIKE AITKEN (HTTP://WWW.NBC-LINKS.COM/POWERPOINT.HTML)

Many PowerPoint® presentations are confusing

or even misleading despite their creator's best efforts. My goal is to help you improve those best efforts. In this book I assume that you've already got a PowerPoint®, Keynote®, or other electronic slideshow presentation or are well on your way toward creating one. This book can help you make your diamond in the rough into a jewel: I show you how to revise a draft quickly for clarity and impact, based on 8 simple, easy-to-use Cognitive Communication Rules. Using this book, you should be able to revise even a complex presentation during a short plane flight.

The 8 Cognitive Communication Rules follow from facts about our human minds, which have predictable strengths and weaknesses. These rules allow you to play to the strengths of your audience members and not fall prey to their weaknesses. Knowing how your audience members receive what you present will always give you an important advantage; after all, you make presentations not to Vulcans, but to humans—cognitive shortcomings and all. But more than that, presentations that play to the strengths of the human mind and avoid relying on its weaknesses are stress-free for the audience, which in turn can make them less stressful for you!

This book builds on two of my recent books, *Clear and to the Point* and *Graph Design for the Eye and Mind*. In these books I reviewed and distilled many years of research into how the mind processes information, and used those findings to formulate the 8 Cognitive Communication Rules. The Cognitive Communication Rules and the recommendations that follow from them are firmly grounded in key facts about perception, cognition, emotion, memory, and comprehension.

GET READY TO ROLL UP YOUR SLEEVES AND EDIT

To be successful, any presentation must achieve three goals: It must connect with the audience members; focus their attention on what is relevant;

and lead them to understand and remember what you have to say. An electronic slideshow is only an aid to your speech, but a poor slideshow can distract from—or even undermine—your intended message. In the following chapters we will review the most common, self-defeating errors and how to fix them.

As you read these chapters and apply them to your own presentations, keep in mind that these recommendations are rooted in more than taste and opinion—they rest on solid facts about how the mind works. I won't bring up the 8 Cognitive Communication Rules every time they apply, but you should try to be aware of them.

To get a sense of these rules, let's begin by looking at the work of a master visual communicator, Gary Trudeau. Here's one of his Doonesbury comics, which you will shortly see in a new way:

FIG 1.1
You will see this comic strip in a new light after understanding the first four Cognitive Communication Rules. DOONESBURY © G.B. Trudeau. Reprinted with permission of UNIVERSAL PRESS SYNDICATE. All rights reserved.

Perhaps this isn't the funniest of his strips, but it's just right for introducing four of the rules. Let's go through it one panel at a time.

The first panel gives you just enough information to know what the strip is going to be about—no more, no less. This panel illustrates the first Cognitive Communication Rule:

1. Goldilocks Rule: To connect with your audience members, avoid presenting too little or too much information, but rather present *just the right amount*. Your audience members will understand and remember your message more easily if the amount of detail you present is appropriate for the point you are making. Joseph Williams, in his superb *Style: Lessons in Clarity and Grace*, formulated the Goldilocks Rule as a guideline for producing clear writing, and it applies equally well to all aspects of communication. In the first panel of the comic strip, Trudeau tells us just enough, no more nor no less, to understand what the strip is about.

You may think that this rule is so obvious that nobody would ever violate it. In fact, some reviewers of my book *Clear and to the Point* made exactly this claim. But I've been looking closely at PowerPoint® presentations for many years, and my experience was different from theirs. So, I decided to do what any scientist would do: conduct a study.

To study common errors in PowerPoint® presentations, my colleagues and I began by using a random sampling technique to download 140 representative PowerPoint® presentations; we took these presentations from five categories: Business, Education, Government, Research, and Miscellaneous fields. Two independent judges evaluated the presentations, noting when recommendations made in this book had been violated (and these judges made very similar evaluations, which shows that the recommendations provided in this book are clear-cut). We decided that even "a single bad apple spoils the barrel," and hence if even a single slide violated one of the recommendations, the whole presentation was scored as having violated both that recommendation and the Cognitive Communication Rule that gives rise to it. Making your audience members work hard to understand even a single slide can lose their attention for the rest of your presentation. Why take the risk?

In what follows, for each of the Cognitive Communication Rules, I'll briefly summarize four aspects of the findings: the overall percentage of presentations that violated the rule, the single worst offense (i.e., particular recommendation stemming from the rule that was violated most often), the frequency of that single worst offense, and which of the five categories (Business, Education, Government, Research, and Miscellaneous) had the most violations of the rule.

RESEARCH RESULTS FOR THE GOLDILOCKS RULE TELL US THAT:

- Overall: 81% of the presentations violated the Goldilocks Rule in at least one slide.
- Single worst offense: Bullets that did not introduce topic sentences or phrases or did not present specific cases or examples. Instead, bullets presented extraneous material, including word-for-word scripts for the

presenter to read aloud. Not only is reading aloud boring, but the audience members can often read ahead, which then interferes with their listening to what the presenter has to say.

- Frequency of single worst offense: 47%.
- Worst category: The Miscellaneous category was the worst, with 91% of the presentations having at least one slide that violated this rule—but Business was not far behind, with 88% of the presentations having at least one slide that violated this rule.

Trudeau's second panel illustrates the second Cognitive Communication Rule. Its visual structure clarifies what Trudeau wants to say.

2. Birds of a Feather Rule: Group information to make it easier to understand. Our brains automatically organize information in particular ways, so it will be easier and faster for your audience members to understand and remember what you present when you organize it appropriately—so their brains can easily form the appropriate groups (such as associating a label with what is being labeled).

For instance, we automatically see visual elements that are near each other as a group: When you see XXX XXX, you see two groups of Xs, not six separate Xs. And when you see XX XX XX, you see the same number of letters as three groups. Birds of a feather flock together—and such flocking in part grows out of how close the elements are to each other (their "proximity"). Our brains also group elements based on other characteristics—in particular, we automatically see visual elements that are similar as a group: When you see **XXX**ooo, you see two groups, not six letters.

In short, words and graphics in your presentation that are near or similar to each other will be grouped together—for better or worse. (In later chapters we'll consider other principles that underlie how our brains group visual elements.)

Now look again at the second panel in the strip. To show people interacting in a static drawing, which is limited to only two dimensions, Trudeau has taken advantage of the two principles of the Birds of a Feather Rule I just summarized: In this panel, the characters not only are shown in the same type of silhouette (so the *similarity* of their forms groups them together), but also are joined at the hip (so their *proximity* also groups them together). By using the two aspects of the Birds of a Feather Rule, Trudeau effectively conveys the sense that these two people are a conversational unit.

RESEARCH RESULTS FOR THE BIRDS OF A FEATHER RULE TELL US THAT:

- Overall: 36% of the presentations violated the Birds of a Feather Rule in at least one slide.
- Single worst offense: Complex tables that were shown with no guidelines to help the viewer organize them into rows and columns.
- Frequency of single worst offense: This problem was evident in 15% of the presentations.
- Worst category: Business, with 50% of the presentations having at least one slide that violated this rule.

The Birds of a Feather Rule also applies to how words in a sentence or phrase are organized. Based partly on proximity, our brains group words according to their roles in conveying a concept. For example, in the third panel of the comic strip, when you see "Mr. Duke, I come from a small, isolated mountain village," the words "I come from" group into one concept, and "a small, isolated mountain village" group into another. We automatically separate these into segments of a story.

When organizing your information, create groups that are clear, are memorable, and help create a story about your topic—groups that will be natural for your audience members' brains to put together as a unit. In other words, use characteristics such as proximity and similarity to define meaningful groups. For example, a slide showing the disposition of troops on a battlefield might make it clear that there are cavalry, infantry, artillery, and support staff—rather than highlighting all the people who are wearing the same uniform. Even if the point of your talk is to group information in a radical new way, for example, separating troops based on blood type or economic class, you should still use these principles to make it easier for your audience members to follow your argument.

A very important point to keep in mind about these groups, or "psychological units," is that we can immediately absorb only about four of them at a time, which brings us to the third rule, which is demonstrated in the third panel of the comic strip.

3. Rule of Four: Present four or fewer groups of items at a time. If you present more than four groups at any one time, you will tax your audience members' cognitive abilities, causing them to confuse parts of your message, forget it entirely, or become fatigued and just tune you out. In short, they will lose patience with you—without knowing why.

That's the bad news. The good news is that when you go into more detail, each of the items in your four (or fewer) groups itself can be a group – and you can include up to four subgroups or elements under each of your original groups, and your audience members generally will be able to grasp and remember them.

For example, look again at the third panel of the Doonsbury strip, where the character says:

> Mr. Duke, I come from a small, isolated mountain village. We
> have no running water or paved roads or health care services. . .

There are two large groups here, which are formed based on the thoughts that are expressed; these two large groups correspond to the two individual sentences. We can easily take in these two large groups. And each of these large groups itself contains groups of concepts. However – effective communicator that he is – Trudeau includes no more than four concepts in each of these large groups. For instance, in the first sentence, `I come from" is the first concept, and the noun `village," plus its modifiers, is the second concept. Because Trudeau's sentence structure follows our natural tendencies, it makes it easy for us to take in and retain the material.

RESEARCH RESULTS FOR THE RULE OF FOUR TELL US THAT:
- Overall: 100% of the presentations violated the Rule of Four in at least one slide.
- Single worst offense: A list of bulleted entries was presented all at once, instead of showing one item at a time. Showing a few bulleted entries at the same time is not necessarily a problem, but showing many at once not only taxes the audience member's capacity to absorb material, but will also be distracting.
- Frequency of single worst offense: This problem was evident in 96% of the presentations.
- Worst category: Every presentation in every category had at least one slide that violated this rule!

This third panel also makes use of the Goldilocks Rule, which sets up the joke. You assume that Trudeau has told you all that's relevant, and hence assume that the village also does not even have electricity. To spring the joke in the fourth panel, Trudeau relies on the fourth Cognitive Communication Rule:

4. Rudolph the Red-Nosed Reindeer Rule: The most important material should look the most important: The audience members will automatically be drawn to what stands out because it has a different color, weight (boldness), size, or movement. As Rudolph's famously unhappy childhood experiences illustrate so well, we pay attention to things that are different.

Now look again at the fourth panel of the comic strip. The villager chastises Mr. Duke, making it clear that his people are not as primitive as Mr. Duke (and we) assume—of course they have a mayor, and of course their mayor uses PowerPoint®! Note that by making the single word `mayor" bold, Trudeau calls our attention to it—an elegant use of the Rudolph the Red-Nosed Reindeer Rule—which springs the joke.

RESEARCH RESULTS FOR THE RUDOLPH THE RED-NOSED REINDEER RULE TELL US THAT:

- Overall: 76% of the presentations violated the Rudolph Rule in at least one slide.
- Single worst offense: The most important content element was not the most salient.
- Frequency of single worst offense: This error was committed in 33% of the presentations.
- Worst category: Miscellaneous presentations were the worst, with 87% having at least one slide that violated this rule.

Remaining Four Rules

I intentionally used Trudeau's comic strip to present just four of the Cognitive Communication Rules: I'm respecting the Rule of Four, which tells us that you, Dear Reader, can't comfortably take in more than four groups of concepts at a time. By presenting the above and now interrupting the flow, proximity will group the four previous rules into a unit. Now let me give you the second set of four rules.

5. **Mr. Magoo Rule:** Text and graphics must be easily distinguished and recognized. Don´t make your audience members feel like the vision-challenged Mr. Magoo—viewers of an electronic slideshow should not risk eyestrain! How many slides have you seen where the text is too small to be read easily? And how many slides have you seen where the background has a striking graphic that competes with the text and illustrations, or where the text is so similar to the background that you need to strain to see it?

The eye cannot resolve details if they are too small, and the brain can detect patterns only when they differ enough from each other and from patterns in the background. Camouflage is nature´s way of fooling the brain, which is useful for potential prey or soldiers in combat but has no place in a slideshow presentation.

RESEARCH RESULTS FOR THE MR. MAGOO RULE TELL US THAT:

- Overall: 100% of the presentations had at least one slide that violated the Mr. Magoo Rule. Yes, *every single one.*
- Single worst offense: All uppercase, all bold, or all italic typeface was used—all of which are difficult to read when used to print more than a few words.
- Frequency of single worst offense: This particular error was committed in 81% of the presentations.
- Worst category: They all qualify as the "worst" category.

6. **Viva la Difference Rule:** Give your audience members new information every time you change something on a slide, such as the color or size of text or the graphics; in addition, indicate every important piece of information by changing the text or graphics.

RESEARCH RESULTS FOR THE VIVA LA DIFFERENCE RULE TELL US THAT:

- Overall: 93% of the presentations violated the Viva la Difference Rule in at least one slide.
- Single worst offense: Visual or auditory characteristics were changed even when they did not signal a change in information. Typeface was the most popular aspect to change for no good reason.
- Frequency of single worst offense: This error was committed in 72% of the presentations.
- Worst category: Education presentations, at 100%.

7. Judging the Book by Its Cover Rule: The form of your message should fit its meaning. For instance, larger bars in a graph should convey larger amounts. We wouldn't be warned not to judge a book by its cover if we didn't do it so often.

RESEARCH RESULTS FOR THE JUDGING THE BOOK BY ITS COVER RULE TELL US THAT:

- Overall: 31% of the presentations violated the Judging the Book by Its Cover Rule in at least one slide.
- Single worst offense: Using a layout that was not consistent with the content. For example, in a stunning violation of one of the most common conventions in Western culture, in some slides time was shown as going from right to left. (This might be appropriate in the Middle East, but not in the United States or Europe.)
- Frequency of single worst offense: This error was committed in 11% of the presentations.
- Worst category: Business presentations, at 53%.

8. Pied Piper Rule: To engage your audience members, lead them by playing a familiar and appealing song: Connect with their interests and what they know. Audience members will follow your presentation better if you give them the information they need to understand the structure of your presentation. And avoid using terms or concepts that they may not know; if they have to think about what a term means, they won't be listening to what else you are telling them. If a new term is necessary, be sure to define it explicitly, and use it in a context where its meaning is clear.

RESEARCH RESULTS FOR THE PIED PIPER RULE TELL US THAT:

- Overall: 70% of the presentations violated the Pied Piper Rule in at least one slide.
- Single worst offense: Using unusual symbols to indicate bullets.
- Frequency of single worst offense: This error was committed in 38% of the presentations.
- Worst category: Business presentations, at 81%.

Although being original is generally a good thing, all good things must be tempered; and being original is not good when it confuses your audience members.

Without question, there´s room for improvement in many PowerPoint® presentations. In fact, *every single presentation* we examined included at least one slide that violated one or more of the recommendations described in the rest of this book! Business presentations were generally the worst offenders, violating an average of 6.7 of the 8 Cognitive Communication Rules, and a *minimum* of 4 of the rules. Given how much is often at stake in business presentations, the frequency of these violations is surprising. However, even in the best category, Government, the presentations violated an average of 5.9 of the 8 rules. These errors are easy to fix, however, so with just a little work, you can easily make vast improvements to your presentation.

Following the Goldilocks Rule, I have now provided enough information to help you develop solid intuitions about how to make electronic slideshow presentations. I don´t expect you to memorize these 8 rules, but rather simply to recognize them when I mention them in the following pages. We´re now ready to go into more detail.

Each of the following chapters starts with a simple checklist to help you identify potential problems. If you answer "Yes" to any question, continue down the list; if you answer "No," go to the correspondingly numbered section within the chapter to see how to revise the relevant material. Every one of these recommendations for revision grows out of the 8 Cognitive Communication Rules just summarized.

Chapter 2

Put Your Message Front and Center

An effective presentation has a clear structure, with a beginning, middle, and end.

Think of the overall structure of your presentation as a pair of bookends surrounding a set of books: The first bookend is the introduction; the books themselves are the body of the presentation; and the final bookend is the wrap-up. An important fact to keep in mind about human memory is that we remember best the beginning and end of a sequence, so the beginning and end of your presentation are particularly important.

Go through the following checklist and consider each of your slides. Questions 1 through 6 address the introduction, 7 through 12 the body, and 13 through 17 the wrap-up. If you answer "Yes" to a question, continue to the next question; if you answer "No," consult the correspondingly numbered section within this chapter to see how to revise your presentation.

INTRODUCTION

1 Do you have a specific message the audience members should understand, believe, and remember?

2 If there is a specific action you want them to take, have you made it clear what it is and why it is appropriate?

3 Do the first few slides define the topic and set the stage for your presentation, as opposed to beginning to develop the specifics of your message?

4 Have you ensured from the outset that your message taps into the audience members' knowledge and interests?

5 Do you tell the audience members at the outset where you are going with the presentation and what you want to conclude?

6 Did you provide an overview of your presentation at the outset?

BODY OF THE PRESENTATION

7 Do you present bridging material that allows you to string your points together into a story?

8 Are you sure that you have precisely the number of slides you need—not too many, not too few?

9 Have you provided specific evidence for your points, and not just abstract principles and generalities?

10 Have you adjusted the level of sophistication and detail so they are appropriate for your particular audience?

11   Have you devised ways to get the audience members actively involved in your presentation (as opposed to expecting them to listen passively)?

12   If you show a dramatic or humorous demonstration or slide, do you move slowly to the next slide?

WRAP-UP

13   Do you conclude by providing a summary?

14   To ensure that the audience members will draw the appropriate conclusions, have you stated them clearly?

15   Do you end your presentation by providing a sense of closure?

16   Do you end your presentation by providing a clear marker that it is over?

17   At the end, do you invite the audience members to visit your (or another relevant) website for notes or further information?

INTRODUCTION

1. Specifying the Message

Before you do anything else, determine your take-home message. What should the audience members believe or know after your presentation? Without determining your message, you cannot know what information is relevant to include or exclude (Goldilocks).

2. Specifying and Justifying the Action

If you want the audience members to take a specific action, you should clearly state what it is – and should organize your presentation to justify why that action is appropriate. If this is the heart of your message, include only information that is relevant for motivating the audience members to take the action you advocate (Goldilocks).

3. Starting with a Bang

Use your very first slide to define the topic and set the stage for your presentation (Goldilocks). To do so, it can provide a title, your name, your affiliation, and any other vital information.

Another effective opening takes two slides:

- First, prepare a graphic that not only defines the topic, but also sets the emotional stage; this slide can greet attendees when they walk into the room. For example, if you are talking about dwindling oil reserves, you could use a picture of oil fields burning in Iraq (Judging the Book by Its Cover).

- Second, make the next slide identical to the first, except that the background is very low contrast and the title of your presentation, your name, and your affiliation are superimposed in clearly discernable type (Mr. Magoo).

When you start your presentation, you can fade the first slide into the second (using the fade transition feature), which is an effective way to grab the attention of the audience members, so that they notice the additional information (Viva la Difference). As shown in Figure 2.1, be sure that the background of the second slide is very low contrast, to make the text stand out (Rudolph the Red-Nosed Reindeer).

4. Tapping into the Audience Members' Knowledge and Interests

Following your introductory slides, which define the topic and set the stage for your presentation, include a slide or slides to tell the audience members why they should pay attention to you. Use these slides to explain why your problem, question, or topic is important to them.

- Craft your message to make contact with what they already know, believe, and are interested in (Pied Piper). For example, if you are going to talk about the price or availability of oil, you can show pictures of long lines at gas pumps, and talk about how fluctuations in gas prices affect ordinary consumers and ripple through the economy at large.

- Sometimes it is useful to start by pointing out an error in how others have addressed your topic, or in common assumptions. This approach can motivate the audience members to pay attention, because nobody likes to be wrong (Pied Piper).

Dance Matters

Diane Dawnett

Reno Dance Associates

FIG 2.1

When transitioning from an opening graphic (top) to a graphic with introductory text (bottom), ensure that the background of the second slide is very low contrast, to make the text stand out.

FIG 2.2

This slide acknowledges that many people have an overly narrow view of what psychology is and believe that it pertains only to psychotherapy. The audience members need to be disabused of this idea early in the presentation.

EXAMPLE: When discussing psychological principles in graph design, I first need to acknowledge that some people have the wrong idea of what a ˮpsychological principleˮ is; they think it has something to do with psychotherapy or Freud. So, to set the record straight, I show a slide with a cartoon of a person on a couch during psychoanalysis with a large red circle with a slash superimposed (Figure 2.2). The slide following the cartoon prompts me to explain what I mean by the term ˮpsychological principleˮ (Figure 2.3). And then I show Figures 2.4 and 2.5. They present the identical data in two different ways, but only in Figure 2.4 is it clear which group is the outlier. Why? Because our visual systems are not good at registering *differences in differences* of height, which is how the relevant information is conveyed in Figure 2.5. But we are terrific at comparing degree of tilt, as in Figure 2.4. Explaining why the first graph shows the outlier group so clearly, whereas the second does not, allows me to illustrate well what I mean by a ˮpsychological principle.ˮ

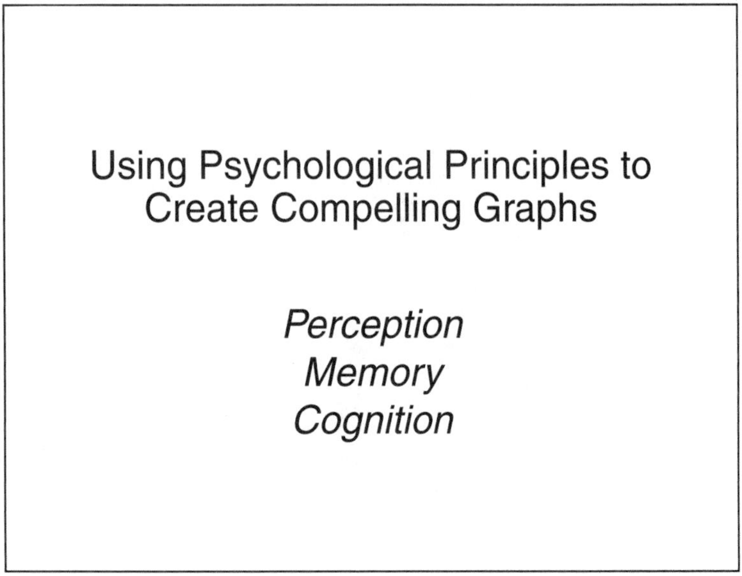

Using Psychological Principles to Create Compelling Graphs

Perception
Memory
Cognition

FIG 2.3

After saying what psychology is not (i.e., entirely focused on psychotherapy), I need to add some of the things that it is; this slide prompts me to explain what I mean by the term "psychological principle."

5. Explaining Your Goals

As part of the introduction, include material that explains what conclusions you are going to support (Goldilocks). Prepare slides, video, or sound—or just a script for what you will say aloud—that will pique the audience members' interest.

Many magazine articles, such as those in the *New Yorker*, do not adopt this advice. Rather, they are discursive or rambling, with the point only slowly emerging, as it does in a novel. But reading such articles is not the same as listening to and watching a presentation. People read for various reasons, including simple entertainment or escape, whereas they expect to be informed by a slideshow presentation. And they expect not to have their time wasted as they are being informed. When you are reading on your own, you can adjust your reading speed, skipping ahead or skimming, but when attending a lecture, you can't make the presenter cut to the chase and get to the point (Goldilocks).

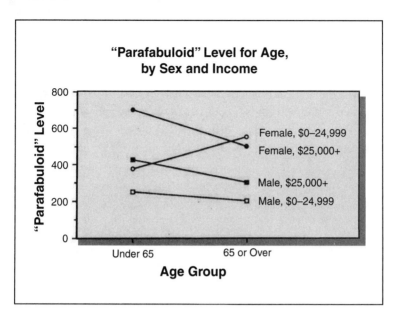

FIG 2.4
The contrasting slope of one line makes the odd group easy to spot; no such visual cue can be given in a table.

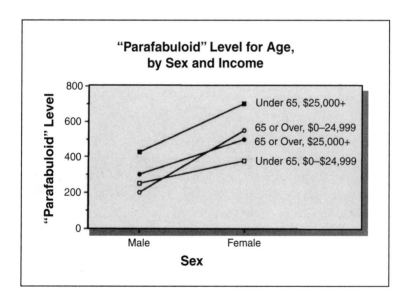

FIG 2.5
This arrangement of the data makes it hard to detect the different trend shown by one group.

6. Providing an Overview

If the structure of your argument involves making distinct points, avoid making your presentation one long string; organize it into digestible modules (Rule of Four). And give the audience members the conceptual structure of the major parts of your presentation so that they can organize what you are going to say. A *brief* outline is a good way to provide this conceptual structure—but so is a diagram, a chart, or even a map if its structure fits the structure of the talk (e.g., you could use a map that shows a highway passing through different cities as an overview if your talk involves a journey, physical or metaphorical—Judging the Book by Its Cover).

> EXAMPLE: In one presentation I literally used a roadmap to provide the conceptual structure. I showed a map of the mythical domain of Middle Earth with a meandering highway marked on it. Five equally spaced locations were marked along this major thorough-fare. Each location was labeled with the heading of a part of the talk, and the headings were ordered from left to right. I started with the leftmost location. To introduce that section, I zoomed in on the heading using the PowerPoint® feature that allowed it to expand until it became very salient (i.e., very eye-catching; Rudolph the Red-Nosed Reindeer). Before each subsequent part of the presentation, I returned to the map and zoomed in on the next location to the right so that the appropriate heading became very salient. The literal map served as a conceptual roadmap, and did so very effectively.

Organize your overview—in whatever form it takes—to reduce the load on your audience members′ perception, memory, and comprehension as much as possible. In a presentation, you force the audience members to keep up with the pace you set; it is not like an article, where the reader can set his or her own pace and go back when desired. Thus, you need to help the audience members follow along so they do not get lost, confused, or overwhelmed.

- Respect the Rule of Four. Organize your outline or graphic into no more than four groups (and each of those groups should include no more than four items or groups of items).

- After you present the overview of the major parts of your presentation, briefly explain what is in each part so that the audience members know what to expect (which will help them to organize the material into digestible units).

BODY OF THE PRESENTATION

7. Telling a Story

The human brain automatically tries to organize and make sense out of experience. And we humans can do this best when we are given information that lets us make connections (Pied Piper). Ensure that you provide such information by telling a story in the body of your presentation. In order to do so:

- Create a clear line of argument from the beginning to the end of the body, along which you build a case for the point or points you want to make.
- Ensure that the transitions between parts are clear. At the beginning of each new part, return to the opening outline or other overview and indicate where you are in the presentation.
- Organize the parts so that each provides the foundation for the next.

8. Using the Right Number of Slides

How many slides should you use? Depending on your material and your audience, you may be able to show a slide every few seconds to great effect, or you may need to dwell on a few for a matter of minutes. Determine the number of slides in accordance with what I call the *Abraham Lincoln principle*. President Lincoln was once asked how long a man's legs should be. His response: Long enough to reach the ground. Similarly, there is no magic number or formula that will tell you how many slides to use. Don't worry about the absolute number of slides you show, but rather show as many (but not more) as you need to be clear and compelling. Use the number of slides you need to reach your particular audience, to ensure that they will grasp and remember your points (Pied Piper). If you don't have time to show as many as you would need, then reconsider your message – you may be trying to cram in too much information in the amount of time you've been given.

9. Providing Concrete, Specific Evidence

For most of us, most of the time, the old maxim still applies: Seeing is believing.

- Present clear, specific evidence to back up your message (Goldilocks). The evidence can be photographs or videos, parts of transcripts or testimonials, depending on what case you want to make.
- Crucially, if you use 3D, animation, or fancy graphics, keep them in the background; put your *message* in the foreground. And resist the temptation to use special effects. Think about science fiction movies with lots of special effects: If you notice that special effects *are* special effects, they will fail. The medium should be so compatible with the message that the audience members don't even notice it (Judging the Book by Its Cover). You and your message should be up front, and the slideshow should be a support; use the slideshow to organize your story and to show evidence.

10. Calibrating the Level

Set the level of sophistication and detail to be appropriate for your audience. In order to know whether you are providing too much or too little information (Goldilocks), you not only need to have determined your message, but also need to get to know your audience (Pied Piper).

- What do you do if you have a mixed audience? When you get to details that are appropriate for the higher end of the group, first say what conclusion you'll draw from considering the details. Following this, explain that you'll take a few minutes to back this up for those who are interested—but that audience members need not be concerned if they aren't following all the details. Then present these details, followed by a reminder of the conclusion.
- But, crucially, don't take more than a few minutes doing this: If you spend too much time drilling deep for the select few, you'll risk inducing boredom in those who cannot follow—which may more than negate any added credibility you gain for those who can. Instead, prepare a handout with additional details (to be passed out only at the end of your talk, so the audience members aren't distracted during it), or – better yet – simply provide a URL to lead the audience members to a website where they can find the details.

11. Involving the Audience

People automatically pay attention to things that are clearly different (Viva la Difference). And there is nothing more striking than being asked suddenly to shift from being a passive listener to being an active performer.

- To keep your audience members alert and engaged, prepare demonstrations that require them to participate.
- To keep your audience members involved, consider asking them to vote (by raising their hands) to indicate whether they agree (or disagree) with a specific point—but only do this once or twice during the presentation (too often becomes tedious).

EXAMPLE: Figures 2.6 through 2.9 show my demonstration of the Rule of Four. Here's how I set it up: When I present Figure 2.6, I tell the

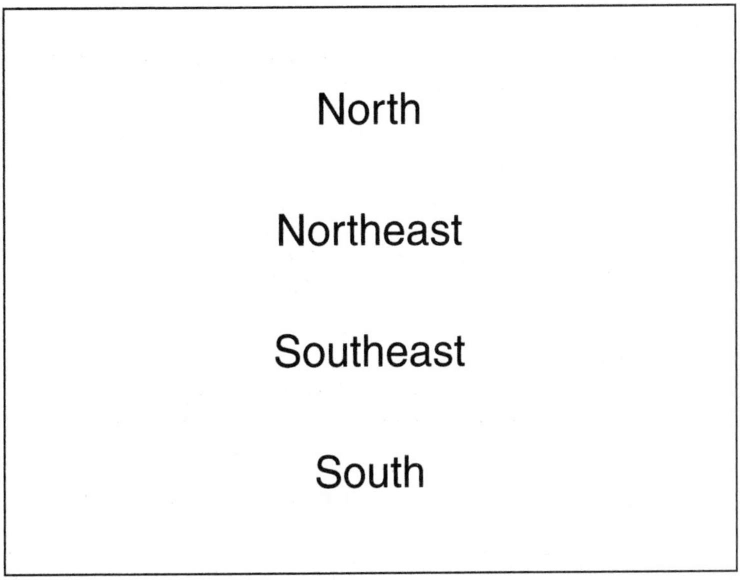

North

Northeast

Southeast

South

FIG 2.6

This slide illustrates the first step of a demonstration to illustrate key characteristics of our limited-capacity short-term memories. I told the audience members that I would read the directions one at a time, and they should visualize a 1-inch line segment pointing in each direction, with each successive segment attached to the tail end of the previous one to form a pathway.

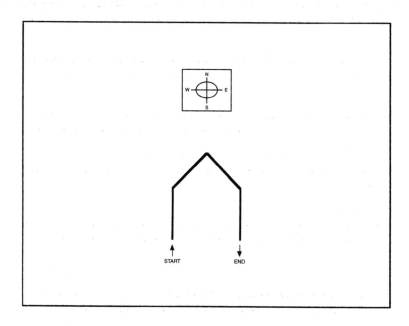

FIG 2.7
This slide illustrates the path that the audience members should have visualized after receiving the directions in Figure 2.6. I used this and the previous slide to teach the audience members the task and to give them a little practice before turning to the actual demonstration in the next two slides.

audience that I'll read a set of directions, such as the ones they see. Then I tell them that I want them to do the following:

- Visualize a 1-inch line segment, pointed in each direction I specify
- Then mentally connect each segment to the end of the previously specified one, creating a path of connected segments

Figure 2.7 illustrates the path that would have been formed by following the directions in Figure 2.6. I then ask whether there are any questions about what they are supposed to do. When their task is clear, I ask them to close their eyes and visualize the pathway while I read aloud each direction in Figure 2.8. I use PowerPoint® to show me each direction, every 4 seconds, which is enough time for the audience members to visualize each segment and add it to the sequence.

After reading the last direction, I ask the audience members to open their eyes and look at Figure 2.9, and to raise their hands if they were able to

```
                    Northeast

                    Southeast

                     North

                      East

                     South

                      East

                     North

                      East

                     South

                    Northeast

                    Southeast
```

FIG 2.8
The actual test directions I used in this demonstration. The audience members were asked to close their eyes and visualize a line segment pointed in each direction, with each line in succession connected to the previous one to form a single pathway.

visualize this pathway. Then I ask them to raise their hands if they noticed the repeating patterns, the peaked and square forms. Finally, and this is the crucial part of the demonstration, I ask how many of those who "got it right" also noticed the patterns. Without fail, virtually all of the people who got it right also noticed the patterns. Why? Because the limit on short-term memory is not the number of items (the individual line segments, in this case)—it's the number of groups. If audience members could figure out how to organize the segments into four or fewer groups, they could store the entire set of 11 directions in short-term memory.

12. Providing Recovery Time after a Dramatic Moment

In a series of items (such as words or pictures), one that stands out is likely to be remembered. For example, if you showed people a list of neutral words (e.g., tree, tire, desk) and then inserted a curse word, people later would remember the curse word better than the others. Moreover, and perhaps more interesting, the items immediately before and after the distinctive one are remembered *worse* than the others; this is a

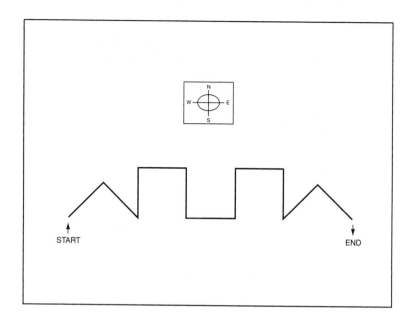

FIG 2.9

The pathway that the audience members should have visualized upon hearing the directions in Figure 2.8. Typically, only people who noticed the repeating patterns got this right, which illustrates that we can hold about four units in short-term memory, and that each of those units in turn can be composed of about four elements.

well-documented psychological phenomenon called the *von Restorff effect* (named after the German scientist Hedwig von Restorff). Our attention is grabbed by the distinctive item, and is grabbed away from those that precede and follow it.

Thus, if you have a particularly dramatic or humorous slide (which makes it distinctive), pause before presenting it and then again before continuing after it—or you run the risk that the audience members won't register what you say before or after it.

THE WRAP-UP

13. Summarizing the Take-Home Message

Make a duplicate of the opening outline or road-map graphic and show it again at the end of the last section of your presentation. Use this slide to organize your summary, briefly noting the main message from each part. (As noted earlier, if your presentation has major parts, present this outline or other type of roadmap before you begin each one, as a transition [Viva la Difference; Goldilocks].) Even if the audience members do not follow every word you say, putting a summary slide at the end of the presentation (and at the end of each individual part) will ensure that they get the thrust of your presentation (Goldilocks).

14. Emphasizing Conclusions

Ask yourself: If your audience members were to give a one- or two-sentence summary of your presentation to a friend, what would it be? Instead of trusting that summary to chance, give it to them directly (Goldilocks). And instead of trusting to memory your ability to reiterate the key points, prepare slides that make these crucial points.

One way to give your audience the message directly is to return to the same graphics that you showed in the introduction to put your presentation in context, but now add some text or verbal explanation to help your audience members to see them "in a new light."

> EXAMPLE: When I discuss the 8 Cognitive Communication Rules summarized in Chapter 1, I often begin by showing the Doonesbury comic strip reprinted in Chapter 1; I then discuss the first four rules (using other examples), and return to the strip after the fourth one—and use the rules to explain how the comic strip works.

15. Providing a Snappy Ending

After your summary, close crisply to signal that you've put in place the final bookend. I can't count the number of times I've heard presentations that ended limply with a statement such as, "Well, that's it" or "OK, that's all I want to say," leaving the audience members wondering whether more should have been said. An effective way to end with a snap is by using a graphic or, perhaps, a well-chosen cartoon (Viva la Difference).

> EXAMPLE: I've given a presentation on the nature of mental imagery in which I stress that we can have mental images from more than one of our senses ("seeing with the mind's eye," "hearing with the mind's ear," and so on). At the end of this presentation, I showed a Dilbert

comic strip. Dilbert was on a date. In the first panel, his date says, "I cannot begin to describe how I feel when I'm with you."" Dilbert replies, "Try." In the next panel, she says, "Imagine a spring day, with bright flowers, birds singing and a gentle breeze." Dilbert is smiling. And then comes the last panel, in which she continues, "And now imagine a tractor on your chest."

After the audience laughed, I returned to the comic strip and noted the different modalities of mental imagery, the visual (flowers), auditory (birds), and tactile (breeze and tractor). I finished with a comment that the author of the strip was not only a keen observer of human relationships, but also a perceptive observer of mental processing, having noticed these important aspects of mental imagery. I then thanked the audience for their attention.

Ending on a crisp note like that left a moment of silence, followed by a gratifying amount of applause (probably as much for my treatment of the comic strip as for the talk itself). (Note: If you have any doubt about whether it is appropriate to show or even describe a cartoon or comic strip, give your lawyer a call—better safe than sued!)

16. Closing the Loop

At the very end, repeat your very first slide, with the title of the presentation and your name—neatly putting in place the second bookend (Birds of a Feather). If you leave this slide on the screen during the question period, it has the added benefit of helping the audience members to stay on topic.

17. Giving the Take-Away

If you presented detailed material that is too dense for the audience members to memorize or write down easily, you can include the URL of your website on the last slide (which should be right beneath your affiliation, under your name – this URL should be part of your identifying information, even when the slide is first shown at the outset). Tell the audience members that they can find the details, and additional supporting evidence, at this site.

Some authors (such as Reynolds and Duarte) recommend passing out a handout at the end of the talk. My advice is different: I recommend sending the audience members to your website, for three reasons:

- Paper is easy to lose, is easy to treat as trash (which may or may not be properly recycled), and requires a clunky hard-copy filing system.
- Sending them to your website gives you another chance to expose them to relevant materials and information.
- Sending them to your website invites them to contact you—which can result in communication at another level than what is possible in a formal setting. (Of course, there can be too much of a good thing—but there are ways to regulate the amount of traffic you need to respond to, if that's a problem.)

Chapter 3

Make Text Clear and Legible

Illegible text has defeated many PowerPoint® presentations. To

spot problems in how you present written words, go through the following checklist and consider each of your slides. If you answer "Yes" to a question, continue to the next question; if you answer "No," consult the correspondingly numbered section within this chapter to see how to revise your presentation.

Do you:

1 avoid all uppercase, all italics, or all bold in more than a few words?
2 avoid using underlining for emphasis?
3 only emphasize a few words?
4 use different typefaces only to convey information (and not just for variety)?
5 use a standard typeface (and not a complex or fancy one)?
6 use a typeface that is without question large enough to be easily seen from the back of the room?
7 use a sans serif typeface (one without little hooks on the letters)?
8 use a serif typeface (one with little hooks on the letters)?
9 select a typeface only after considering its connotations?
10 use only a single typeface?
11 use text that is clearly distinct from the background?
12 ensure that words that are not relevant at a particular point in the presentation have been made similar to the background?
13 have a background pattern that does not make the content material difficult to discern?
14 use a nonwhite background?

1. Avoiding All Uppercase, All Italics, or All Bold

Don't use UPPERCASE, *italics*, or **bold** for more than three or four words in a line; such letters are relatively similar to each other and require more effort to read than does a standard style (Mr. Magoo). If you have done so, replace your typeface with mixed uppercase and lowercase letters, which are easier to distinguish and read than all uppercase, italics, or bold (Mr. Magoo).

2. Avoiding Underlining for Emphasis

Avoid using underlying for emphasis. Underlining cuts off the descending parts of letters such as "p", "g", and "q", which makes them harder to read (Mr. Magoo). Using restraint, replace underlining with:

- italics,
- bold, or
- a color that contrasts with the background and the other words.

3. Emphasizing Only a Few Words

Only emphasize a few words; if you emphasize too much, it will not stand out from the other material—and hence will not in fact be emphasized (Rudolph the Red-Nosed Reindeer).

4. Using Typefaces to Inform

Use the same typeface on all your slides, with three exceptions. Change typeface to:

- emphasize a key fact, term, or concept (Rudolph the Red-Nosed Reindeer),
- specify different classes of information, such as titles versus content (Viva la Difference), or
- group material into distinct classes (Birds of a Feather).

If you change the typeface, the audience members will expect the change to mean something (Viva la Difference), and hence will be confused if it does not.

5. Avoiding Complex or Fancy Typeface

Use simple typefaces, without highly stylized letters or flourishes or "fancy" embellishment. The **letters of highly stylized typefaces** or *ornate typefaces* are more similar to each other than are letters in standard typefaces, and hence they are harder to read (Mr. Magoo).

6. Using a Large Enough Typeface

Don't make those in the back rows squint and strain to see what you've written. Unfortunately, there is no hard-and-fast rule about how large typeface must be: The size of legible print depends on the size of the letters on the screen, the distance of the viewer, lighting, typeface, contrast, and color—as well as whether the viewer has 20/20 vision!

- As a rule of thumb, text should be at least 24 point, preferably at least 28 point (Mr. Magoo).
- You might—very rarely—get away with a typeface as small as 12 point for something like a label on a graphic if you call attention to it with your pointer and read the words or numbers aloud.

- The key to establishing the appropriate size of typeface is not size per se (e.g., as measured by points), but rather "visual angle." Visual angle corresponds to the size of an object in a photo if you measured it with a ruler placed on the photo. Although the actual size of the object remains the same, the farther away the object is, the smaller its visual angle becomes.

If you are really concerned about the size of your type, when you have time it might be useful to use the following—albeit elaborate—procedure to estimate the appropriate size of text with your color scheme and typeface:

1 Take a photo (or ask a friend to take a photo and e-mail it to you) of the projection screen in the largest room where you'll be speaking, as seen from the back row. Upload the photo into your phone, and measure the size of the projection screen as it appears on your phone (which is a way to estimate the visual angle).

2 Type the question "Can I easily read this?" eight times on your computer's screen, forming a column (using double spacing). Set the type on the first line to be 34 point, the type on the second line to be 32 point, the type on the third line to be 30 point, and so on, decreasing the size by 2 points for each line as you go down the column (go down to 20 point)—like this:

Can I easily read this?
Can I easily read this?
Can I easily read this?
Can I easily read this?

3 Now look at your computer screen as viewed through the camera in your phone. Back away from your computer screen, looking at its image as you move farther back. Stop moving when the image is the same size (i.e., has the same visual angle) on your phone as the image of the projection screen in the photo (from the room in which you will be speaking).

4 Put down your phone. From that distance, look at your computer and decide which typeface is too small to be easily read at a glance. Then choose the size 2 points larger, just to be on the safe side.

7. Using Sans Serif Typeface

Typefaces are divided into two general classes, serif and sans serif. Serif typefaces (such as Times and Palatino) have little "feet," brackets, and hooks at the ends of the lines used in the letters; sans serif typefaces (such as Arial and Century Gothic) have only straightforward strokes.

If typefaces are small (e.g., 14 point, in a figure caption), use sans serif instead of a serif typeface; research has shown that the little feet, brackets, and hooks from different letters in a serif typeface can become inappropriately grouped together, making the letters hard to distinguish (Mr. Magoo).

8. Using Serif Typefaces

See Recommendation 7 for a summary of the distinction between serif and san serif typefaces.

- If the contrast or brightness is so low that viewers can barely see the type (e.g., because the presentation must be in a brightly lit room), research results suggest that you should use serif typefaces; these typefaces will be better because the little feet, brackets, and hooks that are present in serif typefaces provide additional cues regarding the identity of each letter (Mr. Magoo).

- However, it's best not to put yourself in this situation in the first place; try to ensure that the contrast and brightness are set to levels that make words easy to read. In most cases, if the typeface is large enough and the contrast with the background is great enough, any standard typeface will be legible.

9. Considering Connotations

Choose a typeface with a style that fits the message of your presentation (Judging the Book by Its Cover). For example, if you are talking about a high-tech product, a clean sans serif typeface (such as Arial or Helvetica) is most appropriate; if you are talking about an event that took place in the 18th century, such a typeface would not be appropriate—but a traditional serif typeface (such as Times or New York) would be.

10. Mixing Typefaces

- Don't mix and mingle typefaces arbitrarily; when in doubt, use a single typeface throughout (Viva la Difference).

- If you choose, you can use one typeface for titles and another for all other labels—but be consistent in how you use the different typefaces (Viva la Difference).

- In addition, you can use a sans serif typeface for small type (e.g., figure legends) even if you are generally using a serif typeface (Mr. Magoo). Again, be consistent.

11. Using Text Distinct from the Background

Lower the contrast of the background to make it, well, "fade into the background," letting your text assert itself in the foreground (Rudolph the Red-Nosed Reindeer).

EXAMPLE: Orange-yellow or gold type on a dark gray background is easy to read, as is white type on any highly saturated "cool" color, such as blue or green, or black type on a very unsaturated pale color, such as light gray. (See Chapter 7 for more detail.)

12. Making Words Fade into the Background When They Are Not Relevant

- To ensure that the audience members' attention will not wander, gray out all parts of the slide but the section you are discussing. By "gray out," I mean switch the color or density so that the typeface is just barely distinguishable from the background, as shown in Figure 3.1 (Rudolph the Red-Nosed Reindeer).
- Present text when it becomes relevant by increasing its contrast to the background (Rudolph the Red-Nosed Reindeer).

13. De-Emphasizing Background Patterns

Ensure that the background does not distract from the content (i.e., the information-bearing lines and regions). In other words, ensure that the background is not so bold or startling that it lures the eye away from the important elements. A background pattern (such as a photograph or design) should be lighter and in less saturated colors than those used in the rest of the display, have few details, and have soft edges (see Figure 3.2; Rudolph the Red-Nosed Reindeer).

14. Using a White Background

If you use a white background, be sure that the room will be at least partially illuminated. A white background in a dark room produces glare,

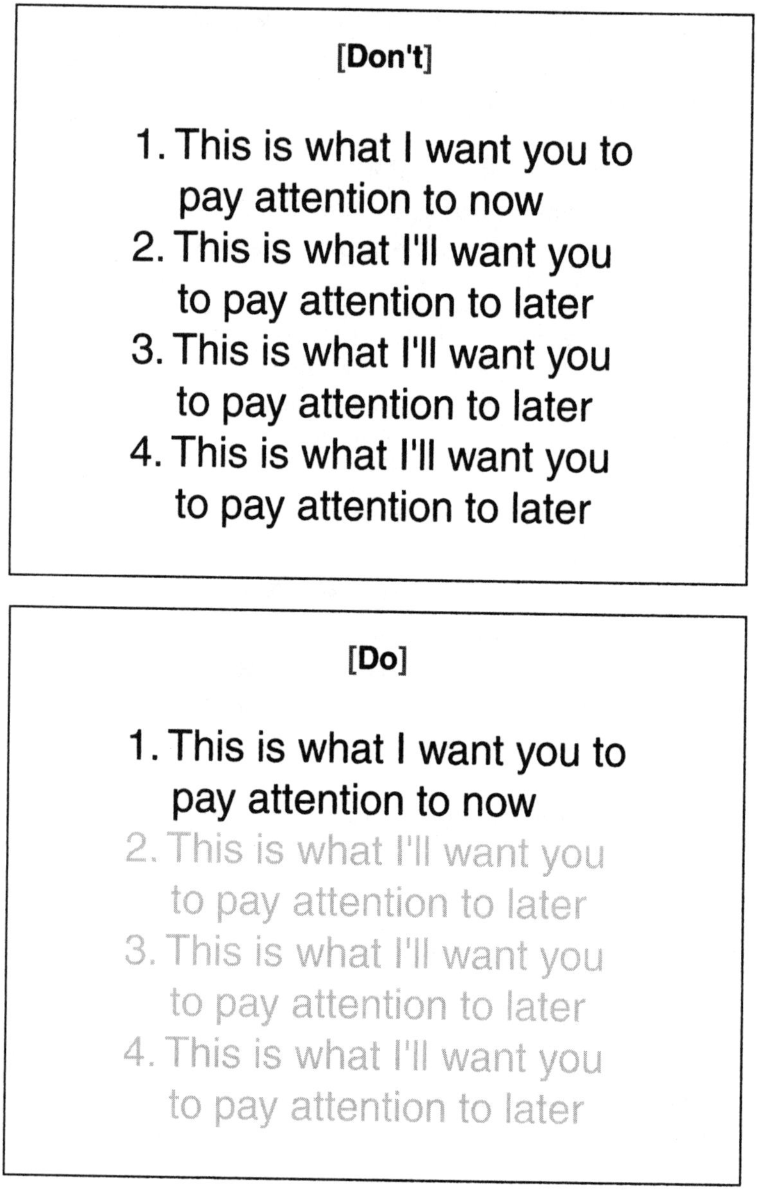

[Don't]

1. This is what I want you to pay attention to now
2. This is what I'll want you to pay attention to later
3. This is what I'll want you to pay attention to later
4. This is what I'll want you to pay attention to later

[Do]

1. This is what I want you to pay attention to now
2. This is what I'll want you to pay attention to later
3. This is what I'll want you to pay attention to later
4. This is what I'll want you to pay attention to later

FIG 3.1

Use graying out to direct the audience members's attention to what is relevant at a particular point in the presentation.

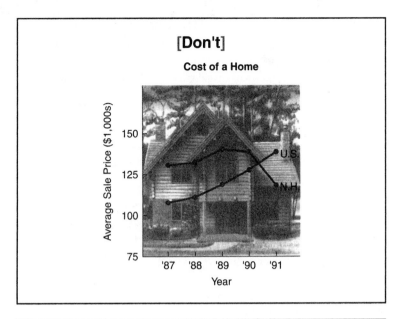

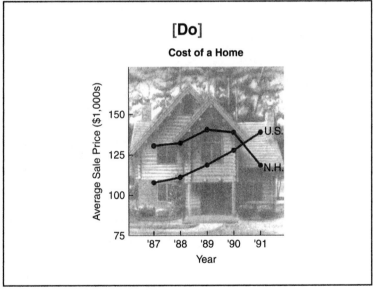

FIG 3.2
If eye-catching characteristics lead the audience members to see the house before the data, they will have to work to sort out the content.

and can result in the audience members´ getting after-images when they move their eyes. To be on the safe side, use a light gray or other light cool color for the background. Alternatively, if you know that you will be presenting in a very dimly lit room, consider using a very dark background with light text and graphics.

Chapter 4

Provide Informative Labels, Titles, and Keys

Labels, titles, and keys serve as crucial guides to the general structure and important points in your presentation. In this chapter we first consider labels in general, then turn to keys (for graphs), and then titles (for slides, graphics, or tables). All of the recommendations made in Chapter 3 also apply here.

Go through the following checklist and consider each of your slides. Questions 1 through 9 address labels, 10 through 14 titles, and 15 through 20 keys. If you answer "Yes" to a question, continue to the next question; if you answer "No," consult the correspondingly numbered section within this chapter to see how to revise your presentation.

LABELS

1 Can labels be read only as having appropriate denotations (direct meanings) and connotations (indirect meanings)?

2 Do all graphics, tables, and other information-bearing parts have labels?

3 Are all labels grouped with the appropriate elements of the display?

4 Are all content elements labeled directly?

5 Are words, numbers, and letters in the same label close together and typographically similar?

6 Do more salient (i.e., eye-catching) labels identify more important parts of the slide?

7 Have you arranged your labels in a clear hierarchy, so that larger or more inclusive categories or entities are clearly seen to contain smaller or less inclusive entities – or so that positions or roles that oversee others are clearly seen to do so?

8 Do you use the same size type and the same typeface for labels of comparable components?

9 Do you use the same terminology in graphics and text?

TITLES

10 Does the title of a slide focus on the most important information?

11 Does the title grab the audience members' attention?

12 Do you present the title of a complex slide before the content elements?

13 Is the title clearly separated from other words or patterns?

14 If a background serves as the title of a slide, does it convey the same message as the presentation?

Using Keys

15 If you have a key, have you used it because you cannot use direct labels (or can use them but doing so will create too much clutter)?

16 Would the slide convey information less effectively if you removed the graphic or table for which you use a key?

17 Is the key at the top right of a single panel or centered over multiple panels?

18 Are the labels and patches in the key easy to tell apart?

19 Are the labels clearly grouped with the corresponding patches?

20 Are the patches in the same order as the content elements they label?

Labels

1. Conveying Denotations and Connotations

Words not only have denotations (direct meanings) but also connotations (indirect meanings), and you need to ensure that both are appropriate for your particular audience (Pied Piper).

EXAMPLE: You could describe a new idea as ˜innovative˝ (which has a positive connotation) or ˜new-fangled˝ (which has a negative connotation). If you are promoting the idea, the connotation of the second term would get in your way.

2. Labeling Content

As a general rule, label everything that is important so that the audience members can read what they failed to hear (Viva la Difference). Even members of the most interested and attentive audiences will space out occasionally.

The only exception to this recommendation is if the identity of a graphic is self-evident; for example, there's no need to label the Statue of Liberty, Eiffel Tower, or Dalai Lama.

3. Grouping Labels with Elements

Ensure that labels are perceptually grouped with the appropriate to-be-labeled entity.

- Place labels nearest to the graphics or other information-bearing elements (e.g., tables) to which they apply (Birds of a Feather).
- Use the same color for a label and the element that it labels (Birds of a Feather).

  EXAMPLE: Ensure that labels of wedges of a pie chart are closest to the to-be-labeled wedge, and—ideally—use a green label for a green wedge, a blue label for a blue wedge, and so forth.

4. Placing Labels Next to Content Elements

- Place labels immediately next to or within content elements, such as objects, bars, lines, or wedges of a pie chart; doing so will allow proximity automatically to group the label with the to-be-labeled material (Birds of a Feather).
- If it is not possible to place a label near what it identifies, or if placing such a label creates clutter, use a key (see sections 15 through 20 later in this chapter; Mr. Magoo).

5. Organizing the Components of a Label

- Place corresponding letters, numbers, and words relatively close to one another (Birds of a Feather).
- Make corresponding letters, numbers, and words the same size, color, and brightness (Birds of a Feather; Viva la Difference).
- Be certain that labels are not so close to one another that they group improperly (Birds of a Feather).

  EXAMPLE: These words group properly. . . These words. . . do. . . NOT.

6. Using Salient Labels

- Make the labels for the most important parts of the slide more salient (more eye-catching), for example by making them large, bold, a striking color, or move in from the side (Rudolph the Red-Nosed Reindeer; Judging the Book by Its Cover).
- As the parts of the slide diminish in importance, make the labels correspondingly less salient (i.e., less likely to grab attention; Rudolph the Red-Nosed Reindeer; Judging the Book by Its Cover).

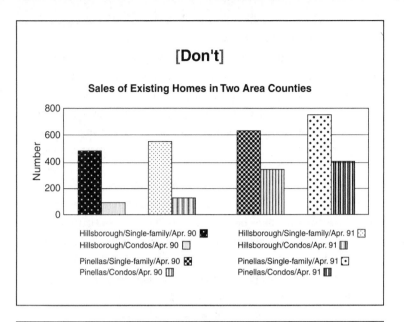

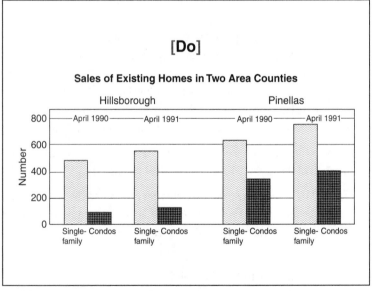

FIG 4.1

Take a look at the two panels labeled ˜Do˝ and ˜Don´t˝ in this figure. Which county had greater sales of single-family homes in 1991, Hillsborough or Pinellas? This answer is relatively easy to determine from ˜Do,˝ but much harder from ˜Don´t.˝ Not only is the display less cluttered when direct labels are used, but also the bars are easier to compare along specific dimensions (dwelling type, county, year) when the labels specify the dimensions separately.

7. Using Hierarchical Labeling

When possible, use a hierarchical labeling system. A hierarchical labeling system is one in which some labels introduce groups of subordinate labels, as shown in Figure 4.1. Labels higher in the hierarchy name larger or more inclusive categories or entities (e.g., as occurs in taxonomies of the animal and plant worlds), or name positions or roles that have greater oversight of others (e.g., as occurs in the military). Use more salient (i.e., eye-catching) labels for more inclusive categories or entities, or for roles and positions that have greater oversight responsibilities; the higher in the hierarchy the label is, the more salient it should be (Rudolph the Red-Nosed Reindeer; Judging the Book by Its Cover). As illustrated in Figure 4.1, `Do,` using a hierarchical labeling system achieves three goals. This scheme:

- eliminates the need for a key (which requires effort to use);
- specifies each of the relevant dimensions separately, which helps the audience members make specific comparisons; and
- allows you to avoid redundant labels, which clutter a display.

8. Selecting Sizes and Typefaces for Components

- Use the same size of type and same typeface when you label the same type of component (wedges, bars, etc.; Judging the Book by Its Cover; Birds of a Feather; Rudolf the Red-Nosed Reindeer).
- Label entities of equal importance with the same typeface, size, and weight (Viva la Difference; Rudolph the Red-Nosed Reindeer).

EXAMPLE: In a graph, use the same size of type and same typeface to label all of the axes, but a larger typeface for the title.

EXAMPLE: If you have two pictures of former CEOs and the sizes of their names or their photos are different, the audience members will draw the obvious conclusion about your level of regard for each.

9. Using Terminology in Graphics and Text

Use the same terms for the same objects in graphics and text. Using different terms in a display and in surrounding text (e.g., bullet points) may lead audience members to wonder whether you mean different things (Viva la Difference).

EXAMPLE: Don't label birds `birds` on a slide while referring to `fowl` in a bullet point (or in your spoken commentary).

10. Focusing on the Most Important Information

- When formulating a title, ask yourself what material you want to stress. Define the focus, and only mention the background or context if it is immediately relevant (Goldilocks).

  EXAMPLE: If a slide presents information specifically about Canada in the last decade of the 20th century, the place and time should be included in the title. If the slide presents information that is supposed to apply to all places and times (such as data about the nature of visual perception, which just happens to have been collected in Canada at that time), don't include this information in the title.

- Mention what's most important first (Judging the Book by Its Cover).

  EXAMPLE: "Effects of mental illness on earnings of men versus women" puts "mental illness" in the foreground and gender in the background, whereas "Effects of gender on earnings in the mentally ill" puts gender in the foreground and mental illness in the background.

11. Making the Title Grab Attention

Make the title grab attention by centering it at the top and making it larger, bolder, a distinctive color, appear first, or slide in from off-screen when the slide first appears (Rudolph the Red-Nosed Reindeer).

12. Presenting the Title Before the Content

If you have a very complex slide, present the title first, with everything else grayed out (i.e., in a very low-contrast typeface) for a second or two, and then make the entire slide visible (Rudolph the Red-Nosed Reindeer; Rule of Four). This procedure will help to orient the audience members to the material.

13. Separating the Title

If the title is near other words or patterns (e.g., in the background), the audience members may group them incorrectly. Avoid this by ensuring that the title is isolated on the slide (Birds of a Feather; Viva la Difference).

14. Using a Background Pattern

- If you have a background pattern (e.g., a very dim photograph), use it as a kind of pictorial label to underline (as opposed to undermine) the message of the presentation (Judging the Book by Its Cover).

- In order to be effective, the background design must reinforce the content of the presentation, as shown in Figure 4.2. To get a quick sense as to whether you are on track, show a couple of friends the background image that you are considering using and ask them to name it with the first word or phrase that comes to mind; this label should be appropriate for the topic (Judging the Book by Its Cover).

- Don't use decorations that convey no information; every element of a display should convey information. Tacked-on elements—such as pictures of the planets or swirls of different colors—will only serve to distract the viewers (Viva la Difference).

USING KEYS

15. Using Keys and Direct Labels

A key has two components: (1) patches of a graphic that correspond to individual components (e.g., to the colors and textures of individual bars in a bar graph, the line segments in a line graph with multiple lines, or the wedges of a pie graph) and (2) labels that identify these patches (e.g., the label for what the corresponding bars, lines, or wedges specify). These patches typically consist of squares that contain different-texture patterns or segments of dashed versus solid lines.

Use direct labels whenever possible (Birds of a Feather). A key requires the viewers to memorize an association between labels and portions of the graphic or table, and then to find those portions in order to identify them—and there's no need to make the audience members work so hard (Rule of Four).

The two exceptions to this recommendation are illustrated in Figure 4.3, `Do":

- Use a key when there are so many wedges, objects, or segments in a small space that it is impossible to label them directly because the labels would not group properly or they would have to be so small as to be illegible (Birds of a Feather; Mr. Magoo).

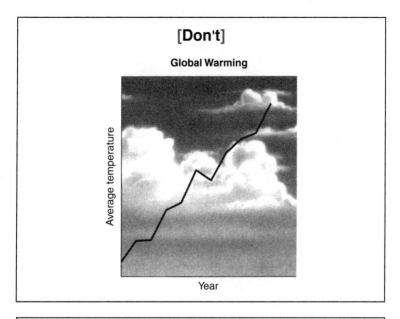

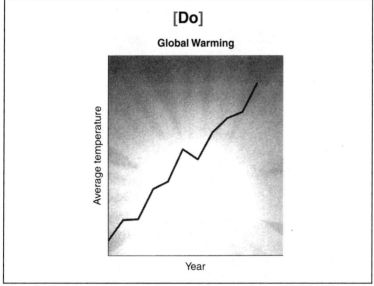

FIG 4.2
The editorial content of a background should not conflict with the message of the display.

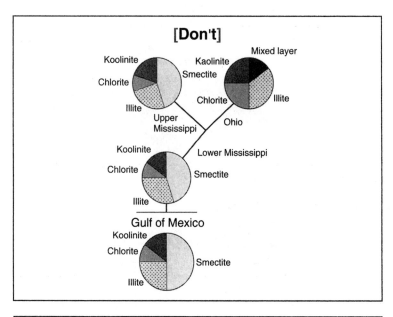

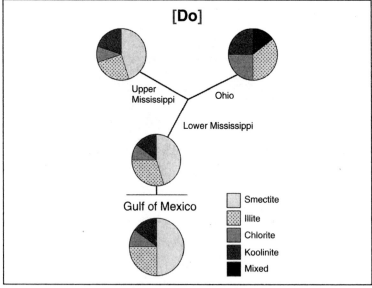

FIG 4.3
A key is sometimes appropriate, particularly when it reduces clutter and allows the structure of the display itself to be more prominent.

50   Better PowerPoint®

- Use a key when the same entities appear in more than two parts of a complicated graphic: The key will reduce both clutter and the difficulty of searching for labels (Rule of Four).

16. Eliminating Complex Graphics and Tables

If you need a key, consider whether you want to show the graphic or table in your presentation to that audience; the display may simply be too complicated to be grasped easily in a presentation (Pied Piper; Rule of Four).

If you do need the graphic or table, consider building up the display a part at a time, so that the key thereby becomes a way to keep track of the separate parts you have shown (Rule of Four).

17. Placing the Key

In a single-panel display, the key is by convention positioned at the top right; in a multipanel display, which contains more than one variant of the same graphic (such as graphs or diagrams), it is centered at the top, directly beneath the title.

If you do not use these default locations, consistently place the key in the same location in all displays (Viva la Difference).

18. Ensuring that Labels and Patches Are Easily Distinguished

Ensure that all labels and patches in the key are easily identified and understood, even from the back of the room or when the lights are turned on (Mr. Magoo).

19. Grouping Labels and Patches

Associate the label and the patch by making sure that they are closer to each other than to any other part of the key (Birds of a Feather).

20. Ordering Patches and Corresponding Content Elements

The patches in the key should be presented in the same order as the corresponding content elements (bars, icons, etc.) in the display itself, as shown in "Do" of Figure 4.4 (Viva la Difference).

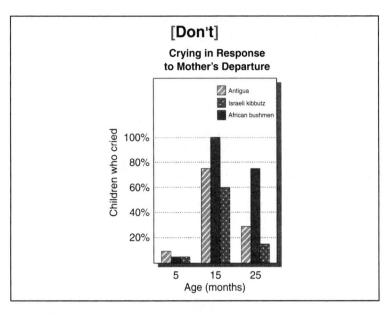

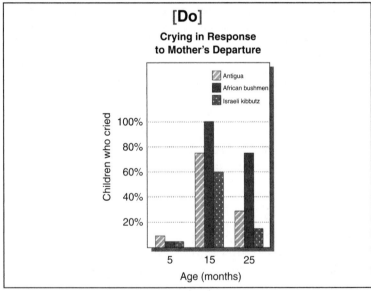

FIG 4.4

Viewers will have to search for corresponding bars if the order of the key does not match the order of the content elements.

Chapter 5

Present Bullets as Nuggets and Landmarks

Bullets are a convenient way to present the

separate elements of a list. However, bullets are a bit like salt—often essential to bring out the best, but distasteful if overdone. As before, go through the following checklist and consider each of your slides. If you answer "Yes" to a question, continue to the next question; if you answer "No," turn to the correspondingly numbered section within this chapter to see how to revise your presentation.

1   Do you show an initial overview of the list of bullets for a very brief period of time?

2   Are you sure that you allow enough time to read (or have audience members read) each individual bulleted item before you go onto the next?

3   Do you present only enough words to convey concepts or examples in the bulleted items?

4   Do you include at most two lines per bulleted entry?

5   Do you include at most four concepts in an entry?

6   Are you certain that you cannot convey your take-home message with less detail?

7   Have you used only single spacing in bulleted lines?

8   Have you used only common, conventional bullet symbols?

9   Do you use only one type of symbol for the bullets?

1. Showing an Overview of the List

Begin by alerting the audience members that you will be presenting a list.

- The most common way to do this is by showing a list of all the bulleted items—but show this list only very briefly, for just enough time to illustrate the length of the list. This will give the audience members a sense of what to expect in what will come.

- Alternatively, you could just mention how many items will be on the list, and start with the first (Goldilocks).

- If you do present the complete list at the outset, it's generally best not to leave it visible as you discuss each item. Ensure that the audience members pay attention only to the first item on your list by graying out everything but this item (making all the other items so faint that they are barely visible). And when you get to the second item, gray out everything but this item, and so forth, as you work down the list (see

Figure 3.1; Goldilocks; Rudolph the Red-Nosed Reindeer). With a short list, research results suggest that you can leave all items visible, but in general you will be better off if you address one item at a time (making sure that you take as much time as necessary to explain fully each one).

2. Presenting Items

Finish reading aloud each item, or pause long enough to allow the audience members to read each item, before you discuss it. And finish discussing each item before you present the next item on the list (Goldilocks). Be sure that you take enough time to explain fully each item before moving on; don't rush it.

In general, it's best to gray out all entries other than the one you are presenting, including the previous one (Goldilocks; Rudolph the Red-Nosed Reindeer). With a short list, this is not always necessary — but it is a good way to ensure that your audience members pay attention just to your current point.

3. Presenting Bulleted Phrases and Sentences

Bulleted entries on a list should provide only key concepts or examples. They should be more like what would have been sent by telegraph in days of old (when each word cost money) than prose. Don't present every word in your entire presentation in bulleted lists (Goldilocks).

4. Presenting Two Lines per Bulleted Entry

As a general rule, include no more than two lines per entry in a bulleted list. Two lines will, on average, specify four concepts, which is as much as people can easily take in and remember at one time (Rule of Four). That said, you can use as many lines as necessary, if you are certain that you have no more than four groups of concepts.

5. Presenting Four or More Concepts

If you have more than four concepts to present, organize them into categories and consider presenting each category on a separate screen (Rule of Four; Birds of a Feather).

If you do this, first present a slide in which you list the categories in the order in which they will be presented, which will prepare the audience members for what is to come (Goldilocks; Pied Piper).

> EXAMPLE: If you want to list 20 types of items commonly found in convenience stores, figure out how to organize them into four or fewer categories, and then divide those categories into four or fewer categories. As shown in Figure 5.1, you might make an initial cut between food items and sundries (with perhaps 12 food items and 8 sundries); then you could divide the food items into four categories (such as candy, vegetables, baked goods, and dairy products) and the sundries into two categories.

6. Eliminating Unnecessary Detail

The advice in the previous recommendation is based on the assumption that each item is in fact important for the point you are making. If the individual items are not important (for instance, it could have been hotdog buns instead of donuts), then you only need to present the categories and list examples of the items. Present no more and no less than the audience members need to know (Goldilocks).

7. Using Single-Spaced Text within Bullets

To be on the safe side, use single-spaced lines within each bullet (Mr. Magoo). We humans can adjust the scope of our attention, for example focusing on a single person's left eyelid or on an entire room. But when we increase the scope of attention to focus on larger areas, our ability to register fine details decreases. For example, if you look at an entire person, you won't register her eyes as sharply as if you just focus on her head. Double-spaced text requires readers to expand their attention over a larger region than is necessary for single-spaced text. This is not a problem when reading on a high-resolution screen or printed page, but a PowerPoint® slide has relatively low resolution. Thus, using double spacing in bullets can increase the difficulty of reading.

8. Avoiding Unusual Bullet Symbols

Use the standard "•" bullet, or for entries within a category, "o" or "-"; a wide range of audience members will have no problem understanding

[Don't]

Socks
Twix
Snickers
Sunglasses
Mars bars
Caps
Carrots
Peas
Squash
Insect repellant
Shoe laces
Shampoo
Bread
Hand lotion
Hotdog buns
Cake
Chap Stick
Donuts
Milk
Ice cream

[Do]

Food Items	Sundries
Candy	*Wearables*
Twix	Sunglasses
Snickers	Socks
Mars bars	Shoe laces
	Caps
Vegetables	
Carrots	*Consumables*
Peas	Hand lotion
Squash	Chap stick
	Insect repellant
Baked goods	Shampoo
Bread	
Hotdog buns	
Cake	
Donuts	
Dairy	
Milk	
Ice cream	

FIG 5.1

If you must present every single item, organize them into categories, each of which should contain no more than four entries. But before doing this, think again: Do the audience members really need to see every one of those individual items? Would selected examples help you to make your point more clearly?

what these symbols signify (Pied Piper). You can use another symbol for a bullet if you are certain that:

- the audience members will understand it,
- the symbol has special relevance to your presentation, and
- the symbol can be clearly read but is not so large as to overpower the text (Pied Piper; Judging the Book by Its Cover; Rudolph the Red-Nosed Reindeer).

EXAMPLE: A small dollar sign might be appropriate if you are listing sources of income.

9. Using More Than One Bullet Symbol

Don't change the shape of the bullets unless you want to signal a change in category. Audience members will assume that any visual change—replacing round bullets with arrows, for example—is intended to highlight something new about the material you are presenting (Viva la Difference).

- To emphasize that you are listing different classes of information, consider using different symbols for bullets (e.g., for income, number of workers, amount of rainfall in different locations) (Viva la Difference).
- To indicate different levels of hierarchy in an outline, consider using different symbols for bullets at the different levels. For example, you might use "•" at the top level (i.e., which specifies the most inclusive category or the role with the greatest oversight), and "○" for the next level down. If you do this, be sure to use the different symbols consistently.

Chapter 6

Include Graphics That Stimulate and Inform

Photographs and clipart practically invite abuse.

Many of us can't resist the temptation to include that cute photo, cartoon, or drawing—and we end up distracting the audience members and undermining our message. Nevertheless, photos and clipart do have their place. Go through the following checklist and consider each of your slides. If you answer "Yes" to a question, continue to the next question; if you answer "No," consult the correspondingly numbered section within this chapter to see how to revise your presentation.

1. Have you used photos or clipart to define the context?
2. Have you used photos or clipart to introduce only concrete (not abstract) ideas?
3. Have you shown photos or clipart with associated text?
4. Have you used photos or clipart to evoke a specific emotion?
5. Have you used photos to present evidence?
6. Have you used photos or clipart to give the audience members time to "come up for air"?
7. Have you used photos or clipart to direct the audience members' attention?
8. Have you checked to see whether you can name the photos or clipart with a word or phrase that bears directly on your point?
9. Is the style of photos or clipart consistent with the tone of your message?
10. Do the illustrations face the front or the center of the screen?
11. Are the graphics sharp and clear (and not grainy)?

1. Defining the Context

Use photos and clipart to set the stage for your entire presentation or a portion of your presentation, or to help you make a specific point (Goldilocks; Judging the Book by Its Cover).

EXAMPLE: A drawing or cartoon of historical figures, such as Benjamin Franklin, can set the stage for a contemporary treatment of a relevant topic—such as ways to make bifocal lenses.

2. Introducing an Abstract Idea

Sometimes very abstract ideas have become associated with concrete icons. Such illustrations can prepare the audience members to organize what you have to say in terms they already know—which is always a good idea (Pied Piper; Judging the Book by Its Cover).

> EXAMPLE: Albert Einstein's face has become a symbol of genius and the Statue of Liberty has become a symbol of freedom for immigrants.

3. Using Text with Photos and Clipart
Include text with photos and clipart to ensure that:

- Audience members will interpret the graphics correctly; many graphics are inherently ambiguous, and text can clarify what the graphics mean in the context of your presentation.

> EXAMPLE: Some years ago a hockey player broke his neck when he slid on his stomach into boards at the side of the rink—he had ducked his head down, right before impact. For weeks afterward, the ice skating rinks around Boston displayed a large poster showing a drawing of a hockey player sliding on his stomach across the ice, with his back fully arched. Under the drawing were the words "Don't Duck." The words made sense of the image, allowing the desired message to stick in the viewers' minds.

- Audience members will remember the key concept you are illustrating.

> EXAMPLE: If you want to remind the audience members of the old saw that "an apple a day will keep the doctor away," you could show a picture of an apple with the words "Doctor Preventative" next to it. Research results show that people remember a picture and associated words better than either one alone.

4. Evoking a Specific Emotion
In some situations, leading your audience members to feel a specific emotion can strengthen your argument (Goldilocks; Viva la Difference). In those situations, choose a slide that evokes a powerful version of the appropriate emotion—and show it to a few people in advance, to be sure that it does in fact evoke the emotion you want. After you present this slide, be sure to let the audience members absorb it before you begin to talk about it.

EXAMPLE: If you want to argue that additional funds should be allocated for the Department of Homeland Security, you might show a photo of a particularly determined-looking, frightening terrorist.

5. Presenting Evidence

Use photos to present evidence for your case. Presenting both text and a graphic will greatly help your audience members to retain the information (Goldilocks).

EXAMPLE: If you have evidence that more people drink tea than coffee worldwide, present multiple separate photos of people from different parts of the world drinking tea, and only one photo of someone drinking coffee. Ideally, you could illustrate the ratio of tea drinkers to coffee drinkers by the number—or relative size—of the corresponding photos.

6. Providing Time to "Come up for Air"

Photos and clipart can also be useful as a break in the steady flow of information, allowing the audience members a moment to reflect and digest. This is especially the case if the photo or clipart is humorous (Goldilocks).

- If you punctuate your presentation with such graphics, be sure that they are relevant to your discussion. If they are not, they will derail the audience members and disrupt the line of your argument (Goldilocks; Viva la Difference).
- Be sure to give the audience members a few seconds to absorb an interlude, so that they are ready to pay attention to your next point (Rudolph the Red-Nosed Reindeer).

7. Directing the Audience Members' Attention

If you've presented mostly text before you present an illustration, the audience members will automatically look at the illustration (Rudolph the Red-Nosed Reindeer). Use this tendency to your advantage, for example by using the image to introduce a new section of the presentation (Viva la Difference).

8. Using Representative Photos and Clipart

If you use photos or clipart to illustrate a specific object or situation, select an illustration of an average, typical example of that object or situation (Judging the Book by Its Cover). One way to discover whether your illustration is appropriate is to ask a few people to name it or describe it; these names or descriptions should correspond to the object or situation you want to show.

EXAMPLE: If you want to discuss the proportion of different sorts of animals that live among humans in urban areas, use an illustration of a pigeon-like bird to illustrate "bird," not a crow or woodpecker.

9. Using Appropriate Styles of Illustrations

Ensure that the style of your photos or clipart is compatible with your message (Judging the Book by Its Cover).

EXAMPLE: Don't use a cute cartoon to illustrate a serious point, and don't use a black-and-white photo to illustrate advanced technology.

10. Facing to the Side

Objects should face the center of the screen. The orientation of the object will direct the audience members' attention (Judging the Book by Its Cover). For example, if you have a face on the right side of the slide looking off to the right, the viewers will have a tendency to do the same—and thus be looking off-screen, rather than where you want them to focus when the next slide appears.

11. Avoiding Grainy Illustrations

Be sure that illustrations do not become grainy if you need to enlarge them to make them visible from the rear of the room (Mr. Magoo).

Chapter 7

Use Color and Texture to Organize and to Emphasize

Almost all information graphics use both color and texture as filling (both in the foreground and the background). To help you evaluate the use of color in your slides, you need some basic definitions. Color is composed of three distinct aspects:

1 *Hue* is the technical term for what we usually mean by color, in other words its qualitative aspect—red, green, etc.

2 *Lightness* refers to the intensity of light reflected off a screen, whereas *brightness* refers to the intensity of light on a monitor. Lightness and brightness can be varied by adding gray.

3 *Saturation* is the depth of the color, which can be varied by adding white, which "washes out" the hue, making it increasingly more subtle, such as in pastel colors.

As usual, first go through the following checklist and consider each of your slides. If you answer "Yes" to a question, continue to the next question; if you answer "No," consult the corresponding section within this chapter to see how to revise your presentation.

1 Have you used four or fewer hues in your text?

2 Are colors clearly distinct?

3 Have you avoided using red and blue, or red and green, in adjacent regions?

4 Do the foreground and background have clearly distinct colors?

5 Are cool colors in the background, and warm ones in the foreground?

6 Does color make more important elements more salient (i.e., more eye-catching)?

7 Is the color of the title more salient (i.e., more eye-catching) than the color of the text?

8 Have you avoided using a heavily saturated blue?

9 Is the same color used for related elements?

10 Are saturation and lightness different when differences in hues are used to indicate different amounts?

11 Have you avoided using hue, lightness, and saturation for different measurements?

12 Have you ensured that colors are compatible with the meanings of the elements?

13 Are you sure that the orientations of the filling lines, which create texture in different regions, are clearly distinct?

14 Are you sure that the hatching patterns in different regions are clearly distinct?

15 Are the orientations of the hatching patterns clearly different, to avoid creating "visual beats"?

1. Avoiding More Than Four Different Colors for Text

Don't be tempted to use more than four colors for your text. In fact, four is probably more than you need: In general, three or even two colors should be sufficient to signal different types of text (e.g., titles versus text; Rudolph the Red-Nosed Reindeer; Rule of Four).

2. Using Colors That Are Clearly Distinct

Adjust the hue, lightness, and saturation so that the colors are clearly distinct.

- To ensure that colors are distinct, separate the hues in your display by at least one other noticeably distinct hue in the spectrum, which can be found in the standard color wheel.
- To be safe, use the "11 colors that are never confused," which are *white, gray, black, red, green, yellow, blue, pink, brown, orange,* and *purple* (Mr. Magoo). But my strong advice is never to use all 11 in a single display: To do so would be overwhelming, making even the word "garish" seem an inappropriately delicate description (Rudolph the Red-Nosed Reindeer; Rule of Four).

3. Avoiding Red/Blue and Red/Green in Adjacent Regions

Do not use red and blue or red and green to define boundaries. Red and blue are difficult to focus on at the same time, whereas it is impossible for many color-blind people to distinguish between red and green (Mr. Magoo).

4. Ensuring That Foreground and Background Have Distinct Colors

Use colors that make the text and graphics in the foreground stand out from the background.

- If the room will be well lit, use dark figures on a light background for maximal ease of reading (Mr. Magoo).
- If the room will be dark, use light figures on a dark background for maximal ease of reading (Mr. Magoo).

- To ensure that colors are easy to distinguish, make them differ in terms of all three qualities: hue, lightness, and saturation (Mr. Magoo).

5. Assigning Colors to the Foreground and Background

Make the text a warmer color than the background. Because of a quirk in how light is focused in the eyes (for details, see my *Graph Design for the Eye and Mind*), "warm" colors, such as red, yellow, or orange, will appear to be in front of "cool" ones, such as green, blue, or violet. So, making the text a warmer color than the background will prevent the background from seeming to fight to move in front of the text (Judging the Book by Its Cover).

Moreover, when two lines cross (as in a line graph), the one with a warmer color should pass over the one with a cooler color; if it does not, the back line will seem to be trying to come forward, trying to snake around the one in front (see Figure 7.1). As entertaining as such effects may be, a good presentation is no place for a visual wrestling match! (Judging the Book by Its Cover)

6. Making More Important Elements Salient

Make the most important element the most salient (i.e., eye-catching; Rudolph the Red-Nosed Reindeer; Judging the Book by Its Cover; Viva la Difference); varying color is one way to control where the audience members look when they first see a slide.

- If no particular element is most important, make the colors equally salient (i.e., equally likely to grab attention; Rudolph the Red-Nosed Reindeer; Judging the Book by Its Cover; Viva la Difference).
- To make elements equally salient, adjust the lightness and saturation until no color dominates (Rudolph the Red-Nosed Reindeer; Viva la Difference). Unfortunately, this must be done based on your subjective impressions: When colors reflect the same objective amount of light, we see blue as the lightest color (or brightest, on a monitor), followed by red, green, yellow, and white. Because our subjective impressions do not line up directly with objective reality, you may need to adjust the colors until they appear comparably salient while still remaining distinct (Rudolph the Red-Nosed Reindeer; Mr. Magoo). If possible, have another person or two check your final product, to ensure that your subjective impressions are shared by others.

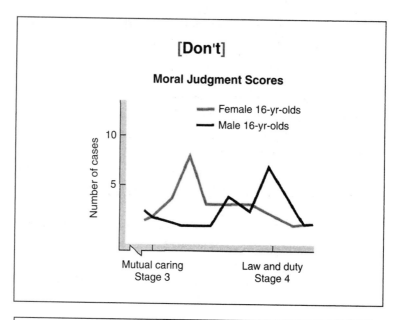

[Don't]

Moral Judgment Scores

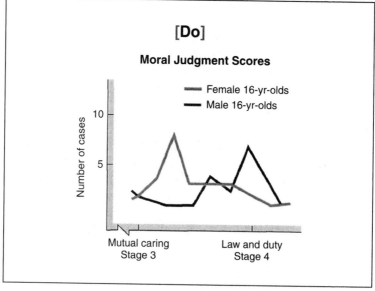

[Do]

Moral Judgment Scores

FIG 7.1

The light line represents a red line; if we could have printed this figure in color, you would see the red line struggling to move to the foreground; this effect is neither esthetically nor functionally desirable.

7. Making the Title Salient

Ensure that the title is a more salient (i.e., eye-catching) color than the text, thereby directing the audience members´ attention appropriately (Rudolph the Red-Nosed Reindeer).

If more than one entry appears beneath a title, you might present the title alone on an initial slide, thereby directing the audience members´ attention to it, and then present each point beneath the title, one at a time (as discussed in Chapter 5; Goldilocks; Rudolph the Red-Nosed Reindeer).

EXAMPLE: You could use crimson on a gray background for titles and a less saturated blue for text entries beneath the title; the color alone should indicate differences in the level of importance (Judging the Book by Its Cover).

8. Avoiding Heavily Saturated Blue

Avoid rendering text or graphics in a deep, heavily saturated blue; this color prevents the eye from focusing on the image properly (it will fall slightly in front of the retina), and hence deep blues appear blurred around the edges (Mr. Magoo).

Similarly, avoid cobalt blue, which is in fact a mixture of blue and red (Mr. Magoo).

9. Grouping Elements

Regions of the same color will be seen as a group (Birds of a Feather), as shown in Figure 7.2.

- Use one color for all titles and another color for all text entries, which will clearly group the material into these two categories.
- Alternatively, use one color for titles, and two other colors for text entries; if you do this, consistently use one color for higher-level entries (i.e., which name categories that include other, subordinate, entries) and the other for subordinate entries—and be sure that the title is in the most salient (i.e., eye-catching) color and the less important entries are in correspondingly less salient colors, according to their relative importance.

EXAMPLE: Grouping by similarity is very useful if you want audience members to compare two or more elements in different places. For

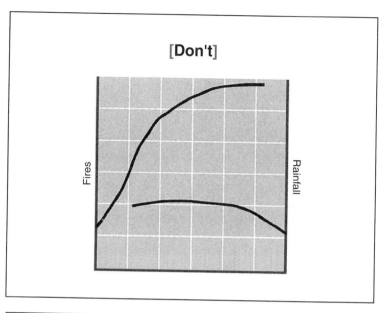

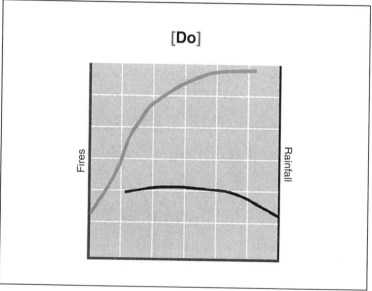

FIG 7.2

If used properly, color can be a very effective grouping device. In the bottom panel, color would effectively group the appropriate scale with the corresponding line if the gray line and left vertical axis were red, and the black line and right vertical axis were blue.

instance, using the same color for corresponding wedges in two pie graphs will group them effectively.

10. Varying Saturation and Lightness with Hues

In general, don't use only different hues to represent different quantities (e.g., using different colors on a map to indicate local temperatures). Using hue to represent quantities requires your audience members to memorize a key because hue itself does not vary along a continuum of less to more. For example, shifting from red to violet does not convey the impression that an amount has been added as clearly as does shifting from a short bar to a tall bar (Judging the Book by Its Cover).

- If you must use hue to convey quantities, use deeper saturations (more color) and greater lightness (more light) for hues that indicate larger amounts. We see increases in both saturation and lightness as having more impact, and so these increases can signal increasing amounts effectively (Judging the Book by Its Cover).
- If you must use hue to convey variations in quantity, use similar changes in color to convey similar increments in the amount. You'll need to experiment to get these amounts even approximately right. Audience members will assume that more similar quantities are conveyed by more similar colors (Judging the Book by Its Cover).

11. Avoiding Using Hue, Lightness, and Saturation for Different Measurements

Don't be tempted to use hue, lightness, and saturation to specify three different types of measurements (as shown in Figure 7.3). A viewer looking at a colored region cannot help but pay attention to its saturation and lightness as well as its hue (Birds of a Feather).

12. Ensuring That Colors Are Compatible with Meaning

Use colors that are compatible with the meaning of the colored graphics or text.

- Be sensitive to conventions of different contexts, cultures, and subcultures (e.g., in a medical context, green indicates infection, whereas in a financial context it indicates profit).

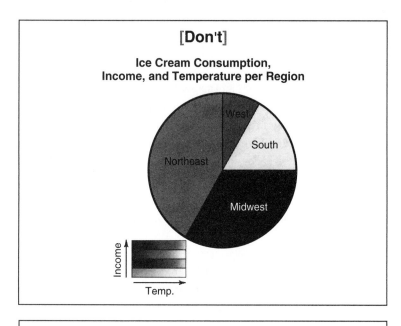

[Don't]

**Ice Cream Consumption,
Income, and Temperature per Region**

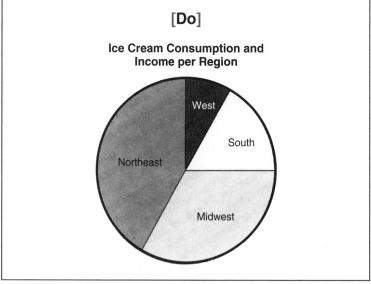

[Do]

**Ice Cream Consumption and
Income per Region**

FIG 7.3

The display on the top uses size to indicate consumption by region, hue to indicate income, and saturation to indicate temperature; it is a puzzle to be solved. The display on the bottom uses only size and saturation to convey amounts, and viewers can clearly sense the orderings here.

- When selecting your overall color scheme, think about the tone you want to set. If you want the audience members to be in a serene mood, use a cool palette; excited, use a warm or even hot palette (Judging the Book by Its Cover).
- Use colors that have connotations that are consistent with your message. For example, research has shown that red and blue have many different connotations in the United States (Judging the Book by Its Cover).

The best survey I know of on this topic was conducted by Joe Hallock (http://joehallock.com/edu/COM498/credits.html). For example, here are some of his survey results, indicating the percentage of Americans who associated blue and red with various concepts.

CONCEPT	BLUE	RED
Trust	34	6
Security	28	9
Speed	1	76
High quality	20	3
Reliability/dependability	43	3
Fear/terror	0	41
Fun	5	16
Favorite color	42	8
Least favorite	0	1

In short, for Americans, blue is generally a more desirable color. But even this depends on the specific message you want to present; if you want to convey speed, fear, or fun, red would be more effective.

13. Making Oriented Lines Distinct

Individual bars in bar graphs, wedges of pie graphs, regions of maps, or portions of diagrams are often filled with a textured pattern. Ensure that neighboring regions have distinct amounts of texture, or the brain will not establish a border between them (Mr. Magoo).

Our visual systems have distinct ˜channels" that allow us automatically to distinguish lines that vary by at least 30 degrees of tilt. As a result, if differently oriented hatchings are used to distinguish regions, their tilts should differ by at least 30 degrees (which is defined by the angle formed by the hands of a clock when they point to adjacent numbers, such as at 12:05; see Figure 7.4) (Mr. Magoo).

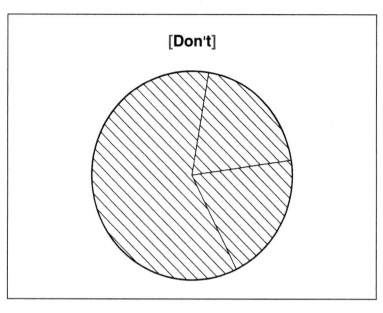

[Don't]

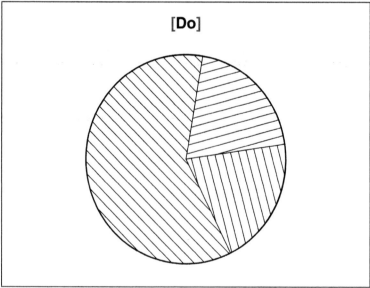

[Do]

FIG 7.4
Line orientations must be immediately distinguished in order to delineate regions clearly.

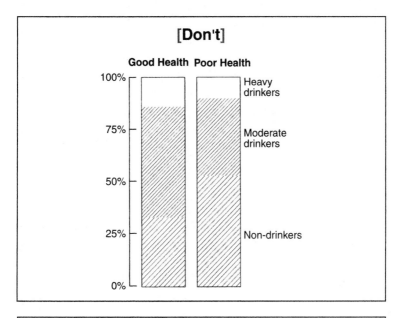

[Don't]

Good Health Poor Health

- Heavy drinkers
- Moderate drinkers
- Non-drinkers

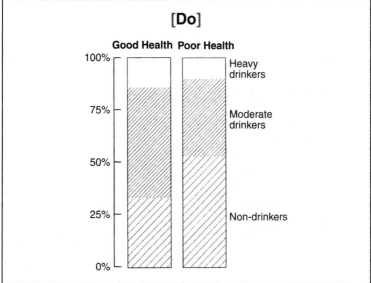

[Do]

Good Health Poor Health

- Heavy drinkers
- Moderate drinkers
- Non-drinkers

FIG 7.5
Line spacings that differ by at least a 2:1 ratio are easy to distinguish at first glance; if regions are not immediately distinguishable, the viewer has to work harder than necessary to compare corresponding elements.

14. Making Hatching Patterns Distinct

If cross-hatching, stripes, dots, dashes, or other regular patterns have similar orientations (that is, within 30 degrees of each other), the densities of the pattern should differ by at least 2 to 1 (as shown in Figure 7.5). For instance, if a region has eight hatch lines to the inch, to be immediately distinguished from it, adjacent regions should have either four or fewer lines to the inch, or 16 or more lines to the inch. Our visual systems function as if they have different "channels" that pick up regions that vary by at least a 2-to-1 ratio of density, and hence those regions are immediately distinguishable (Mr. Magoo).

15. Avoiding Visual Beats

Ensure that the patterns in nearby regions do not seem to "beat" against each other. If the orientations of patterns such as stripes or texture elements are too similar, the patterns may appear to shimmer—a distracting and irritating effect. This effect, shown in Figure 7.6, is likely to happen if the spacing among stripes does not differ by at least a ratio of 2 to 1 (Mr. Magoo).

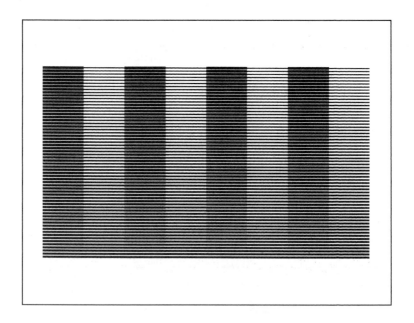

FIG 7.6
An annoying shimmer occurs when your visual system is struggling to detect a poorly defined edge.

Chapter 8

Use Transitions and Animation to Direct Attention

The human brain is wired so that change—including change in location—automatically catches our attention. This makes the movement of a pattern on a screen a double-edged sword: It can be used to direct the audience members' attention to what you want to show, or can distract them from your message. To check whether you are using transitions and animation effectively, go through the following checklist and consider each of your slides. Questions 1 and 2 address transitions, and 3 through 11 address animation. If you answer "Yes" to a question, continue to the next question; if you answer "No," consult the correspondingly numbered section within this chapter to see how to revise your presentation.

TRANSITIONS

1 Do you avoid using special transitions to advance from one slide to the next?

2 If you've used fade-in or fade-out, do your slides fade in or fade out quickly enough?

ANIMATION

3 Have you used animation to direct the audience members' attention to the most important aspects of the slide?

4 Do portions of the same text line or graphic always move together?

5 Are no more than four separate perceptual groups moving simultaneously?

6 Are your audience members only required to read static (and never moving) words?

7 Do complex displays appear one part at a time?

8 Have you ensured that movements are appropriate for what is represented?

9 Are your animations slow enough to be easily tracked, but not so slow as to be boring or easily ignored?

10 Have you avoided using video clips?

11 If you use animation to illustrate the three-dimensional structure of an object, are you sure that your animation is effective?

TRANSITIONS

1. Managing Different Transitions

Many types of transitions are available in PowerPoint®, Keynote®, and other electronic slideshow programs. Such transitions range from simple (such as appearing gradually) to complex effects (such as appearing on a set of rotating blinds). Before changing the nature of any transition between slides, consider the following:

- Don't change the type of transition randomly. Use a novel transition to grab the audience members' attention: Change of any sort should convey information—and novel transitions signal "Wake up and pay attention! This is especially important!" (Viva la Difference).

- Do not make such changes more than once or twice during your presentation; people adapt quickly, so the audience members will soon see frequent change as standard, causing your changes to lose their effect (Viva la Difference).

2. Avoiding Slow Fade-In or Fade-Out

Don't use a slow (i.e., longer than 5 seconds) fade-in or fade-out, because this will lead the audience members to strain at obscure images (Mr. Magoo) and possibly to organize the material incorrectly (Birds of a Feather).

If you are using a slow fade to give audience members a moment or two to absorb complex information, instead simply leave the slide visible until you think they have understood the material.

ANIMATION

3. Directing Attention

In general, construct your slides so that you direct the audience members' attention first to the most important features. Animation is one way to do this, but any manipulation of noticeable characteristics (e.g., size, color) can be effective (Rudolph the Red-Nosed Reindeer).

EXAMPLE: The first panel of Figure 8.1 shows the opening outline I used for a presentation on the brain. The presentation had four

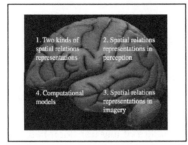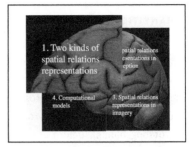

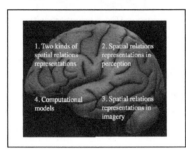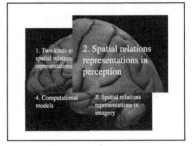

FIG 8.1

The first panel shows the opening outline for a four-part presentation on the brain. To introduce each individual part, I showed the illustration of the brain, and then had one quadrant expand, along with the title of the part. (I've just shown here the results of expanding the quadrant; in the presentation itself, I used animation so that the quadrant seemed to loom up.) I've only shown here the introductions to the first two of the four parts.

parts. To introduce each part, I showed the illustration of the brain and then had one quadrant expand, along with the title of the part. (I've just shown here the results of expanding the quadrant; in the presentation itself, I used animation so that the quadrant seemed to loom up.) Because our visual systems reflexively lead us to attend to visual changes, the audience members were drawn into looking at the title of the upcoming part. The two panels in the top row show how I introduced the first part, and the two panels in the bottom row show how I introduced the second part; I returned to the brain illustration at the beginning of each part, and – with each new part – progressed around it, in a clockwise order.

- If you are discussing a sequence of events that you've represented graphically, use animation to guide the audience members sequentially through the graphic (Goldilocks).

  EXAMPLE: If you present a flowchart, have the arrows appear only when you shift from one phase to another, and then have the arrows literally grow from the part of the chart just discussed to the next one.

- Even if you are not discussing a sequence of events, you can use motion to guide attention: In general, presenting a label first and then having an arrow extend from the label (using the "wipe" feature in PowerPoint®) until it touches the labeled part is an effective way to direct attention (Goldilocks; Rudolph the Red-Nosed Reindeer).

4. Moving Portions Together

Move portions of the same word, phrase, or graphic in the same way, so that the portions group together (Birds of a Feather).

EXAMPLE: If you have each bulleted item in a list enter from the left, ensure that all words in an entry come in together. Having them arrive one at a time, or from different locations, only makes the audience members have to work to organize them into a meaningful unit.

5. Moving Multiple Groups

To avoid overloading the audience members' ability to track and hold in mind information, don't move more than four groups (defined by the Birds of a Feather Rule) at the same time (Rule of Four).

6. Reading Moving Words

Don't require audience members to read moving words. Any gain in visual interest is more than canceled by the added difficulty of distinguishing the words (Mr. Magoo).

7. Presenting Parts of Complex Displays

If you are showing a complex display, you can help the audience members by using animation to build it up, a part at a time (while keeping the portions of each part together, as noted in the previous recommendation; Goldilocks).

For instance, having a part enter from the top or side ensures that the audience members will focus on just that new part, to see how it is integrated into the whole (Rudolph the Red-Nosed Reindeer).

> EXAMPLE: If you were showing a map of the Southern states and wanted to indicate the average annual coffee consumption per capita, you might use icons of stacks of coffee cups to indicate the amount consumed (each cup would signify a certain amount, say ten cups). Each stack would be built up as coffee cups dropped down from the top, one at a time, with the final height indicating the amount of coffee consumed. If the precise amount were important, you could have the numerical value appear at the top of the stack after the cups had slid down to their proper resting places. Using animation in this way will direct the audience members' attention to just the material you want to discuss at any one point.

8. Making Appropriate Animations

Many objects and events have characteristic movements, which you should imitate in how you have them move on the screen (Judging the Book by Its Cover).

> EXAMPLE: If you show a picture of an automobile, don't have it rise up from the bottom of the screen or seem to drop from the sky— have it enter from the left if it faces to the right, or from the right if it faces to the left. Similarly, if you want to use the height of a flower to indicate the amount of rainfall, have the flower grow vertically.

9. Tracking Animations

Animations must not be too fast or too slow.

- Ensure that the animations are slow enough to be tracked easily, without effort; having to pay close attention will wear out the audience members, and—if they bother to keep trying—will irritate them.
- Ensure that the animations are not so slow that they seem interminable. To be effective, they need to grab attention (Rudolph the Red-Nosed Reindeer).

10. Using Video Clips

Use video clips to illustrate an event that unfolds over time (Judging the Book by Its Cover).

- All of the recommendations regarding photos and clipart in Chapter 6 also apply to video clips.

- Be sure that your video will in fact operate on the computer you are using—video clips are memory intensive, and so will not run on all machines.

11. Illustrating Three-Dimensional Structure

One way to illustrate the structure of a three-dimensional object is to use animation to rotate it in depth. The rotation will be most effective if:

- it is as slow as possible while still revealing the overall structure (Birds of a Feather), and

- four or fewer perceptual units are highlighted (e.g., with a distinctive color; Rule of Four).

EXAMPLE: The parts of the human brain are easier to see and organize when a semi-transparent illustration appears three-dimensional (e.g., because it is rotating in depth) than when it is presented in only two-dimensions.

Chapter 9

Add Sound to Alert the Audience and to Paint a Picture

Electronic slideshow programs allow you to present sounds, either from a built-in menu of choices (which in PowerPoint®, for example, includes the sounds of a dog barking and a man laughing) or that you record or download from one of the many resources on the web. Go through the following checklist and consider each of your slides. If you answer "Yes" to a question, continue to the next question; if you answer "No," consult the correspondingly numbered section within this chapter to see how to revise your presentation.

1   If you use sounds to grab the audience members' attention, are you sure they have their intended effect?

2   Have you used sounds sparingly, so that you are sure they will draw attention?

3   If you use sounds to define the context, are you sure that they do in fact evoke the appropriate context?

4   Are you sure that the sounds you use to introduce a slide are appropriate for the topic and point?

5   If you use sounds to allow the audience members to "come up for air," are you sure that they do not disrupt your presentation?

6   Have you used sounds as sources of evidence?

7   Have you been careful to coordinate sounds, text, and graphics?

8   Have you ensured that tonal quality and volume are constant?

9   Have you checked the volume level?

10   Have you ensured that the sound will be high fidelity?

1. Grabbing Attention

Use sounds to alert the audience members to a new event. If a slide has been visible for a few minutes and then you change only a portion of the slide, an appropriate sound will help to draw the audience members' attention to the change (Rudolph the Red-Nosed Reindeer).

EXAMPLE: If you want to show how lightning can start a forest fire, you may first need to show the audience members a picture of a forest and describe the relevant conditions. If this takes you a few minutes, you might then want to present an audible "crack" when you show the lightning bolt.

2. Using Sounds Sparingly

If you use sound to grab attention, do so sparingly. The first time you do this, it will wake up the audience members and alert them to the upcoming event. By the third time, they may be irritated—and may even begin to filter out the sound (Viva la Difference).

3. Defining the Context

Sounds can set the stage for your entire presentation, a portion of your presentation, or a specific point. These sounds should be appropriate for the material and function as a kind of auditory title (Judging the Book by Its Cover).

EXAMPLE: If you are talking about pollution in the seas, you can start with the sound of surf. Or if you are talking about the growing barter economy, you can play the sound of an open-air market. Both National Public Radio (NPR) and the British Broadcasting Corporation (BBC) radio news make very effective use of such sounds to set the stage for their feature stories.

4. Using Appropriate Sounds

If you use a sound to introduce a slide, ensure that it is compatible with the point you are making (Judging the Book by Its Cover).

EXAMPLE: If you want to introduce a presentation or section on the effects of a hurricane, the sounds of a ferocious wind might be appropriate, especially if accompanied by a video clip of the wind ripping through a town. The sounds of gentle rain on a roof would not be appropriate.

- If you use an inappropriate sound, it will seem funny—which is not always a bad thing, but you should intend this effect, not fall victim to it (Goldilocks).
- Never use rude or crude sounds—you know what they are (Goldilocks).

5. Using Sounds to Allow the Audience Members to ˮCome up for Airˮ

Sounds can serve as a kind of punctuation in a complex presentation (again, NPR and BBC radio are very good at doing this). Giving the audience members a chance to ˮcome up for airˮ allows them to process the information you´ve just presented (Goldilocks). However, you should use sound in this way only very sparingly, and your timing must be just right—otherwise your presentation (and you) will run the risk of not seeming serious (Judging the Book by Its Cover).

> EXAMPLE: If you've been presenting data on emerging stock markets in the former Soviet Union, you might have a few seconds of the sound of the floor of one of the exchanges accompanying an appropriate title on a slide, such as "Russian Stock Exchanges."

6. Using Sounds as Evidence

Sounds, especially recorded dialogues, can serve the same roles as photographs when used as evidence (Judging the Book by Its Cover; Goldilocks).

> EXAMPLE: Recordings of former Illinois governor Blagojevich's (you remember him—he was the one who tried to sell President Obama's vacated Senate seat) damning phone calls were powerful evidence against him.

7. Coordinating Sounds, Text, and Graphics

Present sounds with appropriate visuals. If you are presenting sounds as evidence, the ultimate example of coordinating sounds with graphics is a video clip, where the audience members see the sources of the sounds (Judging the Book by Its Cover).

- If the sounds are discrete, such as the sounds different animals make, show a photo of each object, and click on the graphic to present the corresponding sound (Judging the Book by Its Cover).
- If you show animations with sounds, ensure that the sounds are linked correctly with the visuals. For example, even slightly desynchronized lip movements and speech can be very irritating.

8. Varying Sound Quality and Volume

If you use sounds, ensure that they are consistent in tonal quality and volume—unless changing the quality or volume is part of your message (Viva la Difference).

9. Checking Volume Level

Sounds must be loud enough to be heard throughout the room (Mr. Magoo). But don't make the sounds too loud, which not only will cause the audience members to cringe, but may also lead them to anticipate further assaults and so not pay close attention to your message (Rudolph the Red-Nosed Reindeer).

10. Ensuring High Fidelity

Because most computers have poor speakers, sounds can be muddy and difficult to understand. Avoid this problem by ensuring that you have good external speakers with independent amplifiers (Mr. Magoo).

Chapter 10

Use Tables to Organize and Summarize

Tables include lists of numbers or words organized into rows and columns. Go through the following checklist of eight features of tables and consider each of your slides. If you answer "Yes" to a question, continue to the next question; if you answer "No," consult the correspondingly numbered section within this chapter to see how to revise your presentation.

1 If you want to show a set of specific values, have you used a numerical table?
2 Have you used a graph rather than a table to show trends or interactions?
3 Are your tables simple enough to grasp in one glance?
4 Do your tables show only the information needed to make your point?
5 Have you organized your tables according to the most important distinctions?
6 Have you used grid lines?
7 Have you included summary statistics?
8 Have you avoided using pictures or icons as labels?

1. Providing a Set of Specific Values

Use a numerical table only if you need to convey a set of specific numerical values, not when you need to covey differences among values. You will be better off using a graph if your goal is to show that one value is greater than another (Judging the Book by Its Cover).

2. Showing Trends or Interactions

Use a graph, not a table, to present a specific trend (such as increased revenues over time) or a difference between trends (such as increased revenues over time in one part of the world with no such increase in another; Judging the Book by Its Cover).

3. Showing Complex Tables

The only times to present a complex table (which cannot be understood in less than one minute) are when you want to show that a lot of data exist or you want to highlight a single value in context (e.g., by putting it in red; Judging the Book by Its Cover). Don't present a research article in a slideshow. PowerPoint® presentations and research articles have different purposes. In an article, you need to present all the details, so a complex table is appropriate. In a presentation, you need to lead the audience members to understand, believe, and remember your message—and you shouldn't ask them to spend even 3 minutes sitting silently in their seats, pondering the various differences among numbers in a table you present (Rule of Four; Goldilocks).

If you have so many entries that they must be very small in order to fit on a slide, this is a painfully clear signal that your table is not going to be very useful for your audience members (Mr. Magoo). Split the table into two or more slides. If you can't do this, consider using a bar graph to present an average (with some measure of variation, such as the standard error of the mean), rather than a table (Goldilocks).

4. Providing Necessary Information

As the Goldilocks Rule reminds us, present no more (and no less) information than you need to make your point. Keep in mind that unnecessary distinctions can confuse the audience members just as quickly as unnecessary data.

EXAMPLE: If you are not interested in monthly fluctuations, don't present values broken down by month; if you are not discussing gender differences, don't present values separately for men and women.

5. Organizing According to Importance

Organize the table so that the more important distinctions are most evident (Rudolph the Red-Nosed Reindeer; Goldilocks; Judging the Book by Its Cover).

EXAMPLE: If you are presenting data from men and women in two countries and the gender difference is more important for your point than nationality, you would organize the table as on the left of Table 10.1. If, however, nationality is more important, then you would organize the data as on the right.

TABLE 10.1

	Men		Women			USA		Canada	
	USA	Canada	USA	Canada		Men	Women	Men	Women
Measure 1	14	15	12	10	Measure 1	14	12	15	10
Measure 2	10	18	9	10	Measure 2	10	9	18	10
Measure 3	12	14	14	13	Measure 3	12	14	14	13
Measure 4	10	12	10	12	Measure 4	10	10	12	12

6. Using Grid Lines

If you need to present more than two columns and two rows, use grid lines; grid lines will organize the table, helping the audience members to scan it (Birds of a Feather). Use heavier lines to divide the table hierarchically, so that the audience members can easily recognize major distinctions (Birds of a Feather).

7. Including Summary Statistics

If you need to present more than two columns and two rows, the specific values are typically less important than the overall variations over rows and columns. If this is true in your case, then include summary statistics (means or totals) at the bottoms of the columns and right-hand sides of the rows (Goldilocks).

If you use summary statistics, they should be heavier, larger, or salient (i.e., eye-catching) in some other way, such as in color or typeface, than the other entries in the table (Rudolph the Red-Nosed Reindeer).

8. Using Pictures or Icons as Labels

If you use graphics to label entries in a table, ensure that the audience members will easily associate the graphics with the appropriate entries (Pied Piper). People are more likely to name objects consistently if a picture illustrates a "prototypical example" (i.e., an average member) of the category (Judging the Book by Its Cover).

EXAMPLE: If you want to illustrate different kinds of animals that are kept as pets, an average-looking mutt is more likely to be labeled "dog" than a St. Bernard or Pekinese would be.

Chapter 11

Be Clear with Charts, Diagrams, and Maps

Charts, diagrams, and maps primarily specify qualitative relationships—that is, relationships based on characteristics other than number.

Charts are visual displays that arrange information-conveying elements into categories or structures. These structures are usually indicated by lines that connect the elements, but just arranging the elements (such as boxes or even just words) into appropriate groups on the screen may be enough to show the relationships clearly (Birds of a Feather).

Unlike charts, parts of diagrams and maps resemble the things they represent. *Diagrams* are pictures of objects or events that use both pictorial elements and symbols (such as arrows to show movement) to convey information—for example, to show the wiring in your kitchen, the way the Eiffel Tower sways in a strong wind, or the assembly of your new barbeque grill.

Maps are stylized pictures of an area that indicate locations and relations among them (usually in terms of relative distances and routes between locations). By using conventional markings, maps can also provide quantitative information about various locations, such as average temperature, voting patterns, and population distribution.

Go through the following checklist and consider each of your slides. Questions 1 through 8 apply to all three kinds of displays. Questions 9 through 12 apply to charts, such as flow charts or organizational charts; questions 13 through 15 apply to diagrams; questions 16 through 22 apply to maps. If you answer "Yes" to a question, continue to the next question; if you answer "No," consult the correspondingly numbered section within this chapter to see how to revise your presentation.

DISPLAYS

1   Does the display directly support the aspect of your message that you are discussing when you show it in your presentation?

2   Have you included the amount of detail necessary to make your point?

3   Are you sure that all of the symbols, concepts, and jargon will be familiar to audience members?

4   Are you sure that the symbols will be unambiguous for your audience members?

5   Are you certain that the audience members can easily distinguish the content from the background?

6 Have you ensured that components of the display are grouped appropriately?

7 Have you used four or fewer groups of components in each display?

8 Have you used animation to illustrate a sequence of events, and if so, are you sure that you have used it effectively?

CHARTS

9 If you want to illustrate the structure of an object, organization, or event, have you used a chart?

10 If you want to illustrate a sequence of steps over time, have you used a chart?

11 Are more inclusive categories or entities, or positions that oversee others, shown above the categories or entities they contain or the positions they oversee?

12 Are you certain that the layout is appropriate for the subject matter?

DIAGRAMS

13 Have you ensured that the diagram has the appropriate level of detail to convey your point to your audience members?

14 If you used an exploded diagram, have you made the spatial relations among the parts clear?

15 Does your diagram illustrate an object from only one point of view?

MAPS

16 If you have used a map, are you certain that you are using it appropriately?

17 Does the map contain only the amount of information needed to convey your message?

18 Have you avoided varying the size of regions to convey quantitative data?

19 Have you avoided using variations in height and width to convey different measurements?

20 Have you used grid marks if you want to convey specific distances?

21 Have you made the more important routes more salient (i.e., eye-catching) than the less important routes?

22 Have you labeled all important routes and not labeled unimportant ones?

Displays

1. Using Relevant Displays

No matter how attractive a chart, diagram, or map is, it will only get in your way if it does not bear directly on the point you are making when you show it. Move it to a place in your presentation where it will help to convey your message, shelve it for a future presentation, or consign it to the dust bin of history (Goldilocks).

2. Setting the Amount of Detail

Even when the display is appropriate, parts of it may not be. Include in a display only material that is directly relevant to the specific point you are making when you show it. But, by the same token, be sure to include all of the material that is relevant to your point (Goldilocks).

> EXAMPLE: A diagram meant to show the parts of a car that change the motion of the wheels may not be helpful if it also shows many of the car's other systems, as in Figure 11.1a; Figure 11.1b is much better for this specific goal. However, the diagram in Figure 11.1a could be just the thing to use if your point is to show a car's major systems.

3. Using Symbols, Concepts, and Jargon

Be sure that the audience members will be comfortable with the concepts and jargon you use. If you are not absolutely certain that the symbols you use will be clear and straightforward for the members of your audience, state the meanings explicitly (Goldilocks).

> EXAMPLE: When describing a flow chart, indicate whether different shapes—circles, squares, and diamonds—have different meanings (such as an operation versus a decision/branching point).

4. Avoiding Ambiguous Symbols

The same symbol may have different meanings in different contexts. For instance, an arrow may indicate parts to be matched, direction of force, or movement. If there is any possibility of confusion, clarify which meaning you want to convey (Goldilocks).

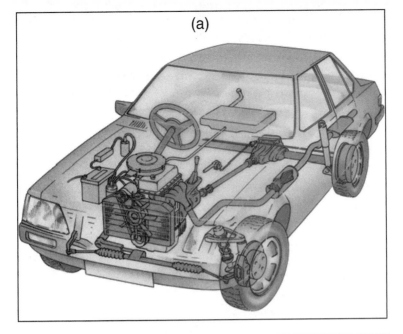

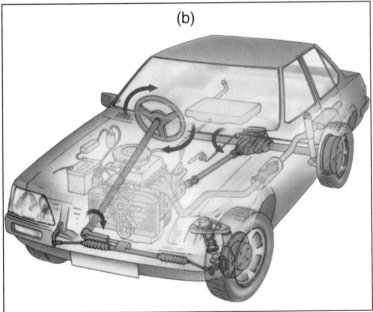

FIG 11.1

If the point is to show the parts of a car that change the motion of the wheels, the top panel is not effective because it contains irrelevant information; the bottom panel is more effective for this purpose. However, if the point is to show the major systems of a car, then the bottom panel would be less effective than the top.

5. Making Illustrations Easy to See

A chart, diagram, or map must have enough contrast with the background to be visible throughout the room, and must be large enough to be legible even from the back row. If it is not, adjust the contrast or size accordingly (Mr. Magoo).

6. Organizing Components

To avoid producing an overwhelming hodgepodge, divide the different aspects of a display into separate perceptual groups (see Figure 11.2; Rule of Four; Birds of a Feather). These groups can be defined by:

- similar shapes,
- similar colors,
- similar shadings,
- similar sizes,
- similar line weights,
- a line or arrow that links objects, or
- locations that produce clusters of objects that are near each other, but which are clearly distinct from other clusters.

In "Do" in Figure 11.2, the phases of the data collection process are distinguished from the evaluation and decision processes.

You can also produce groups simply by presenting a subset of the material at a time, and building up the whole display over the course of a series of slides. To do so, first decide which sets of elements are most closely interacting (e.g., in a flowchart) or most highly related (e.g., adjacent territories on a map), and then present them together.

7. Using Perceptual Groups

If you want audience members to pay attention to more than four objects in your display, devise a way to present them as no more than four groups at a time (using the variables noted in the previous recommendation). The crucial limiting factor is the number of perceptual groups the objects are organized into, not the actual number of objects presented (Rule of Four).

How can you tell how many perceptual groups are present? Fortunately, studies have shown that people are remarkably accurate and consistent at drawing lines around the parts of an object or scene that correspond to perceptual groups. Thus, you should draw lines between

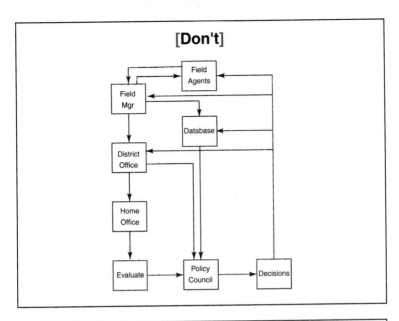

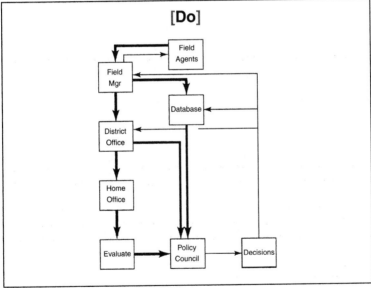

FIG 11.2

A complex chart can be sorted out relatively easily if it is visually organized into components.

parts or groups of objects, which will give you a good sense of the nature and number of groups (Birds of a Feather).

8. Using Animation and Varying Salience

If the point of a display is to illustrate a sequence of events, consider using animation to illustrate it. If you need to vary the speed of the animation, use the "appear" feature (under the "animation" menu in PowerPoint®), which will allow you to define individual frames.

If the display does not lend itself to movement, vary salience—by changing which feature of the display you focus on over time—to guide the audience members' attention (Rudolph the Red-Nosed Reindeer).

EXAMPLE: By systematically changing the colors of specific states of the United States in a series of slides, you could illustrate the course of the Western expansion during the 19th century.

CHARTS

9. Showing Overall Structure in Charts

Use a chart to illustrate the structure of an object, organization, or event. Doing so takes advantage of the Judging the Book by Its Cover Rule; relationships such as "is a member of," "follows," "works for," and "is descended from" are illustrated clearly by the spatial relations of the entities in the display.

10. Showing a Sequence of Steps in Charts

Use a chart (such as a flowchart) to show a sequence of steps over time. Electronic slideshow programs let you show even complex sequences of events by building up a chart a part at a time (Judging the Book by Its Cover).

11. Illustrating More Inclusive Categories or Positions that Oversee Others

Place the symbol or name of larger or more inclusive categories or entities higher in a chart, and then place the symbols or names of smaller or less inclusive categories or entities beneath the larger ones that contain them (Judging the Book by Its Cover). Similarly, do the same for individuals or entities that oversee other individuals or entities (e.g., as might occur in an a hierarchically organized organization, such as the military, universities, or hospitals).

EXAMPLE: Mega Corp. has automotive, consumer electronics, and ranching divisions. The structure of the company could be symbolized at the top of a chart by the name, box, or other symbol that represents the company as a whole, with three names, boxes, or other symbols— one for each division—in a row directly beneath it, and then directly beneath each of these would be names, boxes, or symbols for their components.

12. Using Appropriate Layout in Charts

Respect the convention in Western culture and make a sequence over time proceed from left to right. However, also make sure you respect the specific conventions of your audience members for a specific topic.

EXAMPLE: Computer programmers have developed a specialized sub-culture, in which flowcharts are often presented from the top down, and diamond shapes indicate when a decision is made, squares indicate when a process occurs, and circles indicate when input or output occurs. Similarly, a chart detailing the command structure of an organization should start at the top and work down, as in "Do" in Figure 11.3; it should not go from left to right (Judging the Book by Its Cover).

DIAGRAMS

13. Setting the Amount of Detail in Diagrams

Ensure that you present no more or no less material than is needed to make your specific point (Goldilocks), keeping in mind the background knowledge of your audience members (Pied Piper).

14. Using Exploded Diagrams

If parts of an object are partially concealed in a drawing, and you want to make their shapes or spatial relations very clear, move parts away from the whole. Be sure to use an arrow or other visual means to indicate clearly where each part fits in the whole object. In addition, because the brain processes shape and spatial relations in separate systems and may not combine the two very accurately, show parts near their actual locations in the object depicted, as in "Do" of Figure 11.4 (Birds of a Feather).

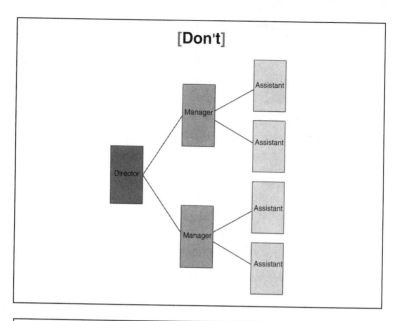

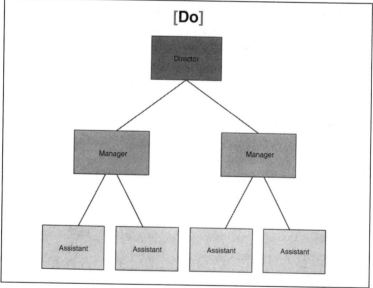

FIG 11.3

Category inclusion and command structure both correspond to vertical spatial relations because some categories or positions are "over" others.

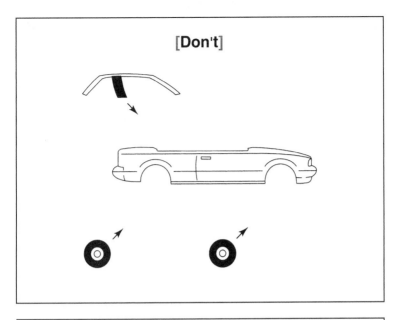

[Don't]

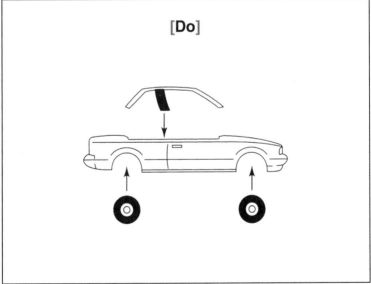

[Do]

FIG 11.4

If spatial relations are distorted to show components, the distortion should be easy to reintegrate; otherwise, viewers will have to expend effort to see the components in place.

15. Illustrating Viewpoint in Diagrams

In any single diagram, show all parts as seen from the same point of view. The brain is wired to assume that an object is seen from only a single vantage point, so your audience members will be confused if you show an object from more than a single point of view—and may not make the effort to reorganize the display on their own (Birds of a Feather).

Similarly, use the same number of dimensions for the whole illustration; for example, if one part is drawn in two dimensions, don't tack on a part drawn in three dimensions.

MAPS

16. Using Maps

Use a map if:

- the relative distances between landmarks or angles of turns are important,
- you want to show how to reach a destination from a number of different starting places, or
- you want the audience members to compare specific values you specify for different locations (Judging the Book by Its Cover).

EXAMPLE: If the population for different parts of a region is presented (perhaps by bars—with higher ones specifying more people— standing on particular locations), the audience members can see not only the relation of population to specific landmarks, such as rivers or the sea, but also the pattern of population variations as a whole.

17. Setting the Amount of Detail in Maps

Include no more or no less information than the audience members need in order to understand your message (Goldilocks).

EXAMPLE: If you want to illustrate how to get to the nearest fire station from Harvard Square, don't include every road in the region (Figure 11.5). Instead, illustrate the roads that are possible routes between the two locations, providing key landmarks to guide the traveler (Goldilocks).

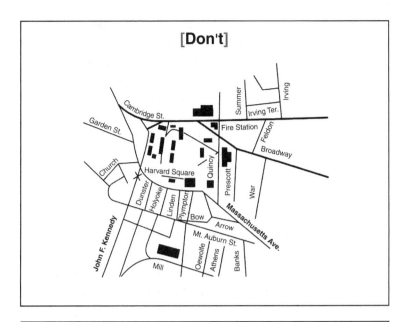

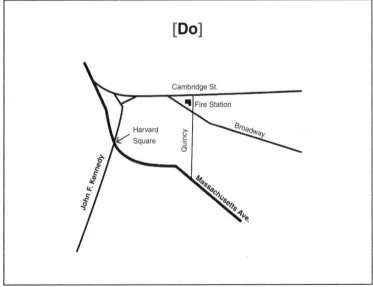

FIG 11.5

A map that includes too much extraneous detail for its purpose is not helpful; to specify the location of the firehouse relative to Harvard Square, only the efficient routes are necessary.

Moreover, if distance per se is not crucial, but the sequence of turns is, there is no reason to draw the map to scale. If you decide not to draw it to scale, however, indicate when distance has been compressed. You can indicate compression with the same sort of truncation marks used to indicate that a Y axis in a graph has been altered (i.e., a pair of short diagonal lines slashing across the route line). This symbol has the advantage of probably being familiar to most people, but because some audience members may not be familiar with the conventions for indicating truncation, be sure to explain what such symbols mean.

18. Varying Sizes of Regions in Maps

Do not vary the sizes of regions of maps, as in "Don't" in Figure 11.6, to show relative rates or quantities, such as per capita beer consumption, number of murders, and so forth. We humans are not very good at estimating area and have trouble comparing relative areas of differently shaped regions. In addition, varying the size of a region to convey information can make the shape of the region unrecognizable, as happened in the "Don't" example of Figure 11.6. At best, such maps convey only a rough impression of rank ordering, and fall short if actual amounts or even precise ordering is to be conveyed.

The human visual system is good at comparing relative length, so a better way to convey amount is to draw a bar, stacked set of icons, or similar symbols at each location, varying length or height to convey quantity.

19. Varying Height and Width in Maps

Don't vary a shape's height and width to specify values of distinct dimensions. The map in "Don't" of Figure 11.7 uses the height of the markers to indicate the population and the width of the markers to indicate the mean temperature of each location. But our brains register the overall area of the markers, not the horizontal and vertical dimensions separately (Birds of a Feather).

20. Using Grid Marks in Maps

Some maps are used to indicate the relative locations of regions or the locations of specific routes, or to provide other kinds of qualitative

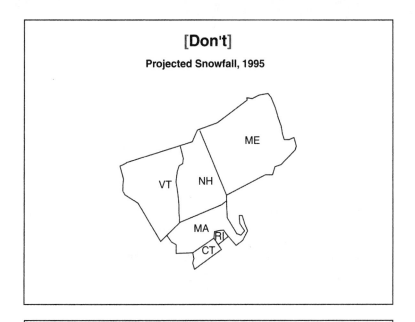

[Don't]

Projected Snowfall, 1995

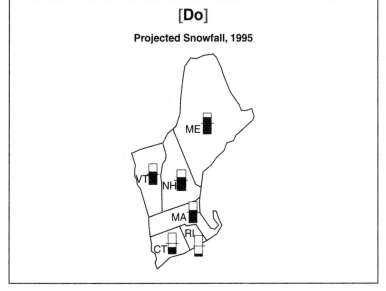

[Do]

Projected Snowfall, 1995

FIG 11.6

It is almost impossible to extract relative amounts from differently shaped areas, even if they are familiar and not distorted. Vary extent along a line or bar instead (the framework around each bar and the short horizontal lines are designed to help viewers compare the black bars).

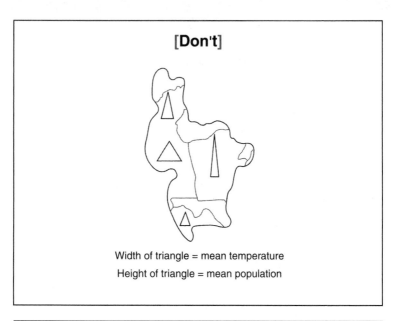

[Don't]

Width of triangle = mean temperature
Height of triangle = mean population

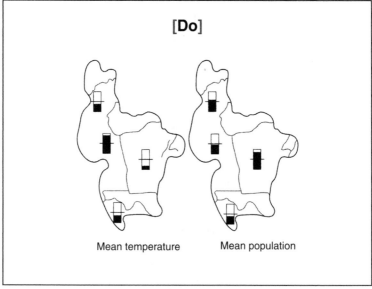

[Do]

Mean temperature   Mean population

FIG 11.7
If both the width and height of the triangles are varied, we see neither variable very well; it is far better to use two different displays, one for each variable.

information. Other maps, however, specify the actual distances between locations. In these cases, grids marks are useful if:

- grid lines are relatively thin and light (not heavy and dark, as in "Don't" of Figure 11.8; Rudolph the Red-Nosed Reindeer; Mr. Magoo);
- more tightly spaced grid lines occur when greater precision is required (Golidlocks);
- heavier grid lines are inserted at equal intervals when grid lines are close together, to help viewers organize and search through the display (Birds of a Feather);
- inner grid lines pass behind the lines, bars, or other objects in graphs or diagrams, which makes them easy to distinguish from the grid (Mr. Magoo); and
- the scale of a map, which is a kind of key that pairs a line length with a unit of distance, should correspond to one or more of the units used to separate the grid lines. If it does not, audience members will have to reorganize the unit line length and mentally divide it into the corresponding lengths on the grid (Birds of a Feather).

21. Showing Important Routes on Maps

Ensure that the most important routes are visually more salient (i.e., more likely to grab attention)—using color or line weight—than less important routes (Rudolph the Red-Nosed Reindeer; Judging the Book by Its Cover). Use the most important routes as the backbone of the map, as in "Do" of Figure 11.9, allowing other routes to be organized by them.

22. Labeling Distances on Maps

If you want the audience members to know the distances between specific pairs of locations, draw lines between them to indicate routes, and directly label the lines with the distances. Do not label unimportant distances (Goldilocks).

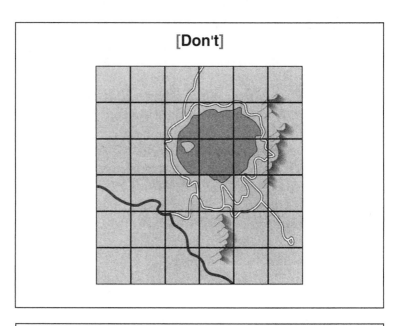

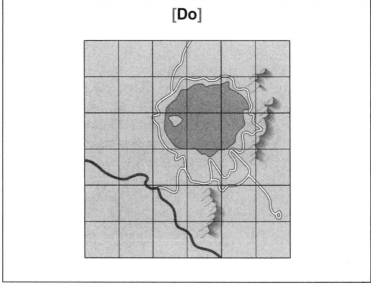

FIG 11.8

If precise distance is not important, there is no reason to include grid lines; if grid lines are included, they should not obscure the features of the territory.

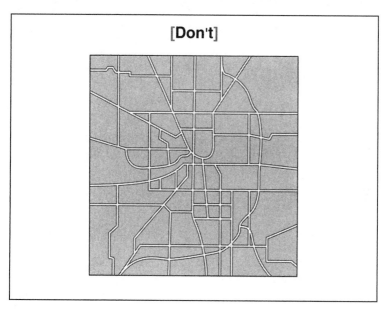

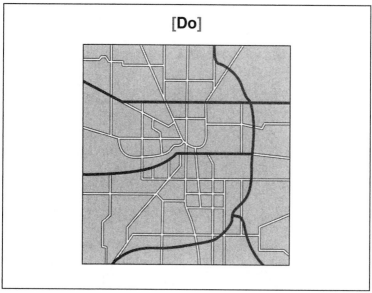

FIG 11.9

Making the major roads correspond to more visually striking lines will help viewers to organize the map as well as to find the most efficient routes.

Chapter 12

Make a Point with Graphs

Graphs convey quantitative information

, such as the number of people who voted in the last dozen elections, the price of tea in different parts of China, or changes over time in the temperature of the pacific ocean. Like other pictures, graphs can be worth a 1,000 words. But sometimes they confuse more than they clarify, and so are not worth even a single word.

Let me begin with a very general observation, which applies to all graphs: In a presentation, you should only show a graph to make a specific point. Your job is to convey a message clearly and convincingly, and you should show a graph only if it helps you accomplish this aim. Always ensure that any graphs you show imply a clear conclusion—and don´t leave it to the audience members to infer what it is: Tell them the point directly when you show the graph.

In this chapter we consider specific characteristics of effective bar, line, and pie graphs, which should be familiar to most audiences members. Bar graphs and line graphs rely on an L-shaped framework, where one axis (typically the X axis, which runs along the bottom) indicates what has been varied or selected; the other axis (typically the Y axis, which is vertical and on the left) indicates the measurements. In contrast, a pie graph (aka a `pie chart´´) is a circle that illustrates how a whole is divided into constituent parts.

Go through the following checklist and consider each of your slides. Questions 1 through 9 apply to both bar and line graphs, questions 10 through 14 apply to bar graphs only, questions 15 through 19 apply to line graphs only, and questions 20 through 24 apply to pie graphs. If you answer `Yes´´ to a question, continue to the next question; if you answer `No,´´ consult the correspondingly numbered section within this chapter to see how to revise your presentation.

Bar Graphs and Line Graphs

1 Have you used a bar graph to show differences between specific point values (and not trends or interactions)?

2 Does the X axis show a discontinuous scale (rather than a continuous one, which would be used for a variable such as time)?

3 Does the X axis show a continuous scale (rather than a discontinuous one, which would be used for a variable such as names of cities)?

4 Do you want to illustrate simple differences among values (and not a trend or trends over a continuous scale)?

5 Do you want to illustrate simple differences among values or a trend (and not an interaction between the entities on the X axis and another variable)?

6 Have you avoided using a mixed bar/line display?

7 Are you certain that the meanings of the axes are clear?

8 Are the labels short enough to fit under a vertical display?

9 Have you used inner grid lines?

BAR GRAPHS

10 Do bars appear in a single set, rather than grouped into separate clusters?

11 If you have clusters of bars, are the bars arranged in the same way in each cluster?

12 If you have clusters of bars, is the space between bar clusters larger than or equal to the width of one bar?

13 Are the individual bars equally salient (eye-catching)?

14 Do the tops of the bars fall within the measurement scale, rather than sticking above the end of the scale?

LINE GRAPHS

15 In a line graph, do lines show data that are equally important?

16 Are lines clearly distinct (and not crossing, or near other lines)?

17 Are you using only solid lines (with no dashes)?

18 If the lines connect dots or symbols, are the dots or symbols more salient (eye-catching) than the lines?

19 Do different lines connect the same type of symbols (e.g., all circles)?

PIE GRAPHS

20 Have you used a pie graph to illustrate relative percentages of parts of a whole?

21 Are only approximate values important (and precise values are not important)?

22 If you have an exploded pie, have you used it to emphasize a few segments?

23 Can you arrange wedges in only a single way?

24 Are you using only a single pie (and not multiple pies)?

Bar Graphs and Line Graphs

1. Showing Differences between Specific Values

The audience members will assume that different bars correspond to specific values, so use a bar graph to contrast specific values (Judging the Book by Its Cover).

2. Using a Continuous Scale on the X Axis

The audience members will assume that a continuous line corresponds to continuous measurements, so if the X axis (which names the things that were varied or selected to be measured) shows a continuous scale, use a line graph (Judging the Book by Its Cover).

3. Using a Discontinuous Scale on the X Axis

If the X axis (which names the things that were varied or selected to be measured) shows a discontinuous scale, you can use either a line or a bar graph if only two values (e.g., men and women, north and south) are plotted. But if the X axis shows a discontinuous scale (e.g., it runs from 1 to 40 and then jumps to 80 to 120, rather than running continuously from 1 to 120), and you have more than two values on it, use a bar graph rather than a line graph.

EXAMPLE: Look at the ˮDon´tˮ version of Figure 12.1, in which the line makes it appear as if the income for consulting partners is accelerating rapidly. This visual impression is less striking in ˮDo.ˮ If the intervals of space along the X axis don´t specify a continuously varying scale, a line will give a misleading impression.

4. Showing Trends over a Continuous Scale

Use a line graph to display trends over a continuous scale, such as time. The continuous rise and fall of a line creates a shape, which we easily interpret as a trend—up, down, or varied (Judging the Book by Its Cover). The yearly pattern of a young man´s fancy is more clearly perceived from ˮDoˮ than from ˮDon´tˮ in Figure 12.2.

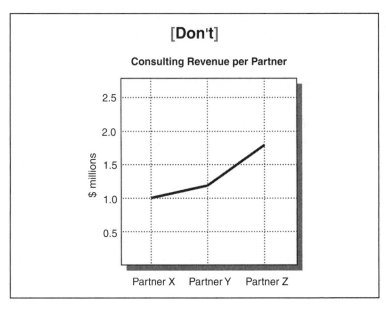

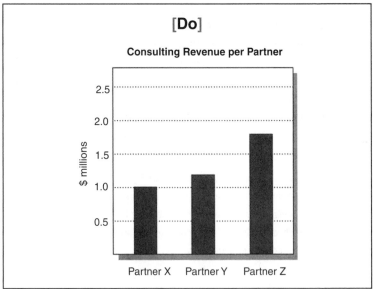

FIG 12.1
A line graph for these data inappropriately suggests a rapid rise along a continuous variation.

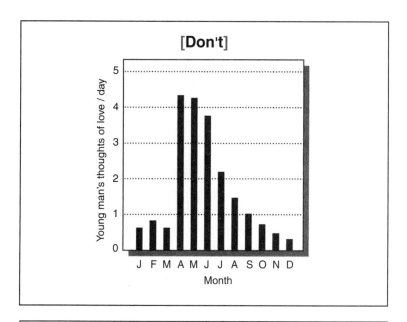

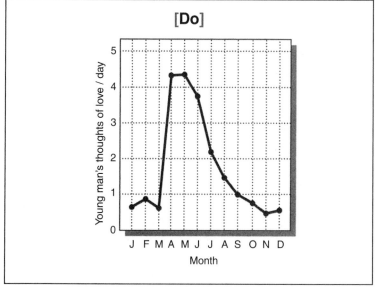

FIG 12.2

The continuous variation of a line is compatible with the continuous variation of time; if you want the audience members to note precise point values, put dots or symbols along the line.

5. Showing Interactions

Use a line graph to display interactions. By "interaction" I mean that the effects of one variable modify the effects of at least one other variable. When describing an interaction, you would say that the effects of a value of Variable 1 depend on the value of Variable 2. For instance, the difference between the average temperature in June and January depends on whether you are in Toronto or Sidney. This interaction between month and country reflects the fact that the value of one variable depends on the value of the other. The visual appearance of crossing lines links neatly into the underlying concept (Judging the Book by Its Cover).

Because most experienced graph readers can immediately recognize patterns as conveying meaning (such as seeing crossing lines, as in Figure 12.3, as showing a type of interaction), a line graph can also be useful if you have two values on a discontinuous scale—provided that the labels or context make it clear that the scale is not continuous. For instance, you can use a line graph even if the X axis conveys rankings (e.g., quartiles) or names (e.g., of companies or cities) if you use clear labels to guide the audience members (Viva la Difference).

6. Avoiding Mixed Bar/Line Displays

Don't use mixed bar/line displays to show interactions. As is evident in "Don't" in Figure 12.4, it is more difficult to see interactions if a mixed display is used because bars and lines don't group to form simple patterns; for easiest comparison of trends and interactions, use multiple lines (Birds of a Feather).

7. Interpreting Ambiguous Axes

Ensure that the X and Y axes are clearly identifiable (Mr. Magoo) and appropriately labeled (Goldilocks; Viva la Difference). The audience members should immediately be oriented to the X axis (which typically indicates what is varied or selected to be measured) and the Y axis (which typically specifies the actual measurements).

8. Fitting Labels under a Vertical Display

If labels are too long to fit under a standard bar graph, you can:

- abbreviate them. But keep in mind that if you do so, you need to ensure that the abbreviations will be easily understood by all members of the audience (Pied Piper).

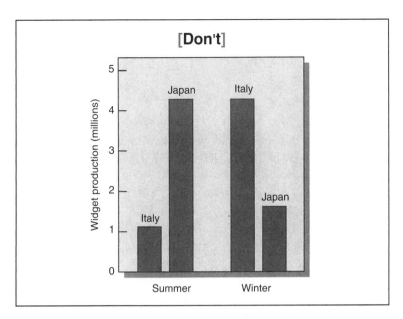

[Don't]

Widget production (millions)

Japan — Italy

Italy — Japan

Summer   Winter

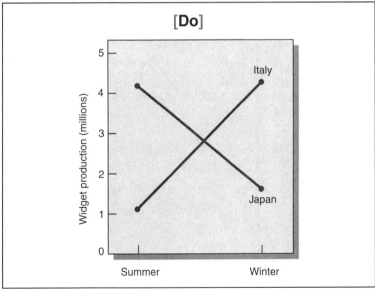

[Do]

Widget production (millions)

Italy

Japan

Summer   Winter

FIG 12.3
Experienced graph readers can interpret typical patterns of lines at a glance. Hence, it is good—especially in a presentation when viewers may not have much time to decode a display—to make use of familiar patterns to convey interactions.

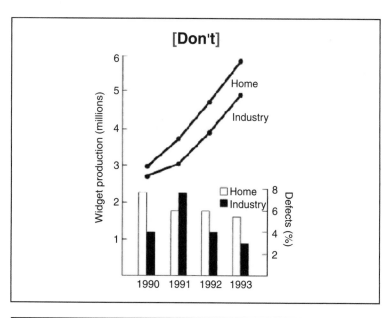

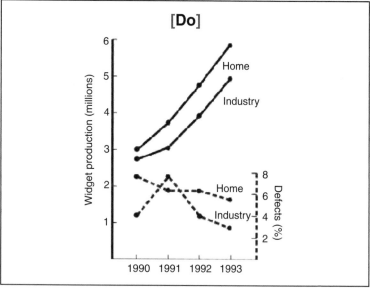

FIG 12.4

The trend toward decreasing number of defects with increasing production, especially for the industrial widget, is not immediately evident from the mixed line/bar display; the visual system more easily groups different lines into a pattern than it groups lines and bars.

- use a horizontal bar graph—where the bars go from left to right and hence the typeface can be large enough to be clearly legible (Mr. Magoo). But if you use a horizontal bar graph, always be sure that the axes are clearly identifiable (Mr. Magoo) and clearly labeled (Goldilocks; Viva la Difference). This is especially important for horizontal bar graphs, because they are less common than vertical ones (Pied Piper).

9. Using Inner Grid Lines

Use an inner grid when precise values are important. For all variants of line and bar graphs, include an inner grid if you want the audience members to be able to see clearly one or more specific values, which can be read off the Y axis more easily if the eye can trace along grid lines (Birds of a Feather).

EXAMPLE: The line graph in Figure 12.5 illustrates a special case in which grid lines are particularly helpful. Look at the vertical difference between the lines over 2 and those over 5. Which difference looks larger? In fact, they are the same distance apart, as you will see if you use the grid lines to compare the two differences. Our visual system tends to register the minimal distance between the lines, not their difference in height; grid lines help the viewer to focus specifically on the vertical extent itself.

BAR GRAPHS

10. Using Clusters of Bars

If you have more than one cluster of the same bars, as in Figure 12.6, be sure to mark in the same way the corresponding bars in each cluster, as in "Do" (Viva la Difference). Try to compare the performance of the two brands of Coca-Cola in 1989 from the "Don't" graph in Figure 12.6. This is not as easy as it should be because—in a misguided attempt at variety in the way the bars are shaded—the designer used different shadings for corresponding elements (Birds of a Feather; Viva la Difference).

11. Arranging Bars in Different Clusters

Arrange corresponding bars the same way in all clusters (Birds of a Feather; Viva la Difference).

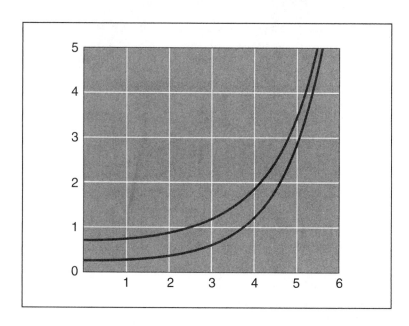

FIG 12.5
Without an inner grid, it is almost impossible to tell that the lines have the same difference in value on the Y axis over the 2 and 5 values on the X axis.

EXAMPLE: Say that you want to graph numbers of young and old male and female voters for each of two counties. The county would be on the X axis, and four bars, one for each of the four demographic groups, would sit over each county. The demographic groups—young men, old men, young women, old women—could be indicated by different shading. The order of the bars for voter groups should be the same for each county, as in "Do" in Figure 12.7. If it isn't, the audience members will not organize them correctly, and so will struggle to make comparisons.

12. Putting Space between Bar Clusters

Leave space between bar clusters so that the bars within a cluster are grouped (Birds of a Feather). Notice how much easier it is to compare the market shares in 1985 for the three brands in "Do" versus "Don't" in Figure 12.8. Group bar clusters over each appropriate location on the

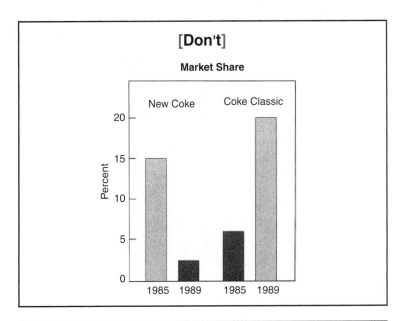

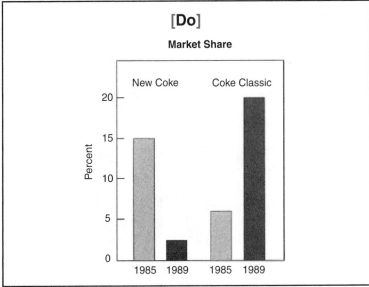

FIG 12.6
Inconsistent marking creates inappropriate groups of bars in "Don't," making it harder to compare corresponding elements.

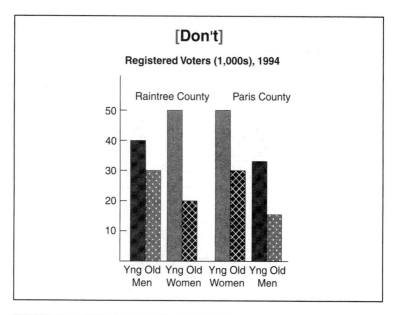

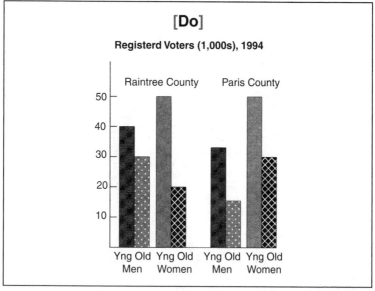

FIG 12.7

A gratuitous change of order makes it difficult to compare corresponding bars.

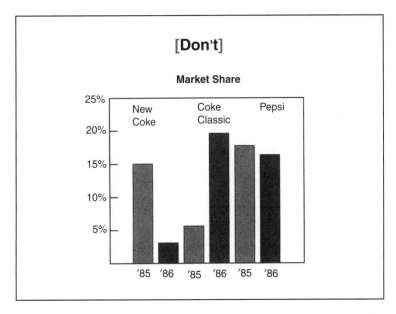

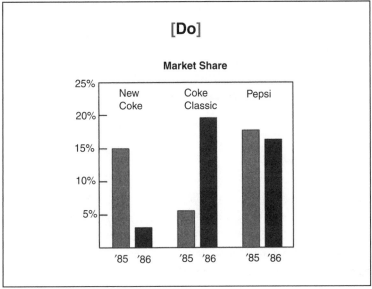

FIG 12.8

Six perceptual units are too many to apprehend immediately; proper grouping not only makes the display easier to take in, but also helps to group the bars with their labels.

X axis and leave extra space between the clusters. As a rule of thumb, the space between clusters should be equal to or larger than the width of one bar (Mr. Magoo).

13. Adjusting Bar Salience

Unless the emphasis is intentional, which is not the case in "Don't" in Figure 12.9, no bar should stand out from the others. If it does, the difference in salience will lead the audience members to notice it first and assume that it is more important than the other bars in the display (Rudolph the Red-Nosed Reindeer).

14. Aligning Bars with the Measurement Scale

Don't extend bars over the top of the Y axis, as in "Don't" in Figure 12.10 (or to the right of the X axis in a horizontal bar graph), if the audience members are to extract specific point values to compare the bars to the scale (Goldilocks). However, if the point of the display is not to show specific values—but only to indicate that, say, housing prices have gone through the roof—you would just be adding extraneous details by including tick marks, labels on the Y axis, and so on. Make the appearance fit the message (Judging the Book by Its Cover; Goldilocks). Some of the most effective graphs in *Time* magazine have tall bars that extend into the text, driving home the point that some trend has exploded beyond its usual boundaries.

LINE GRAPHS

15. Making Lines Look Important

Vary the salience of lines to indicate relative importance (Rudolph the Red-Nosed Reindeer; Judging the Book by Its Cover). Audience members will notice the most salient (because of its striking color, size, or other eye-catching characteristic) line first and interpret it as the most important. In Figure 12.11, if you are looking at all three networks' morning shows and comparing their ratings, the graph on the top is the style you want. But if your subject is NBC's "Today" and you want to emphasize that show's ratings against the other two shows in the field, the one on the bottom better illustrates your focus.

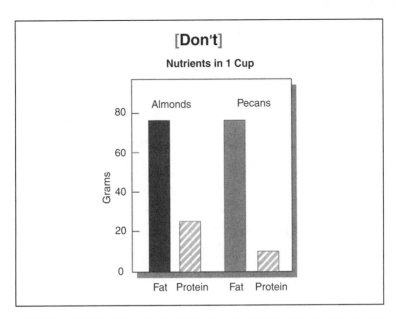

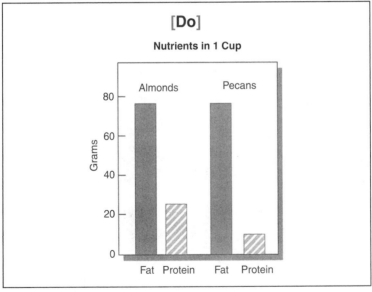

FIG 12.9
Making one element more salient (i.e., eye-catching) will put it at the center of attention. If you want to emphasize that element, this is appropriate; but if you are simply trying to provide visual variety, as in the top panel, it is likely to confuse the audience members.

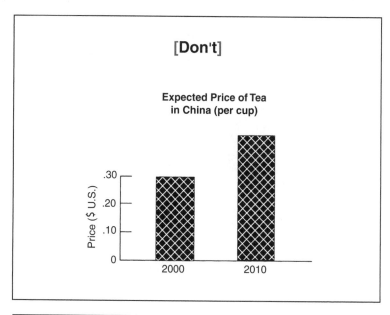

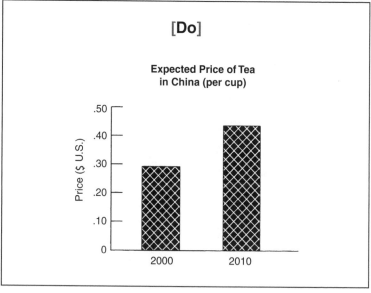

FIG 12.10

If the Y axis is too short ("Don't," at top), the viewer cannot immediately estimate the price of tea in 2010.

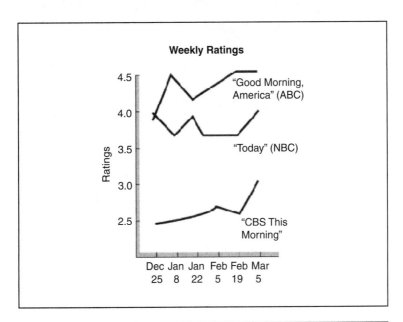

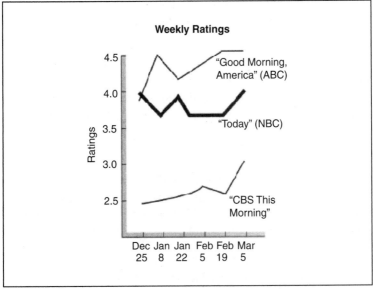

FIG 12.11

If the focus is on NBC, the graph on the bottom is preferable; the increased salience (i.e., eye-catching qualities) of the line for NBC immediately draws the viewer's attention.

16. Ensuring That Crossing or Nearby Lines Are Distinct

Ensure that crossing or nearby lines are clearly distinct. When lines are nearby or cross often, special care must be taken to ensure that segments of one do not become grouped with segments of another (Birds of a Feather). You can make it easier for the audience members to tell lines apart by:

- using different colors or
- using dashed lines (and vary the dashes).

In either case, make sure that the salience of the lines does not vary arbitrarily (Rudolph the Red-Nosed Reindeer; Judging the Book by Its Cover).

17. Using Dashed Lines

To be immediately distinguished from one another, dashed lines should differ in elements per inch in a ratio of at least 2 to 1 (Mr. Magoo). For example, if one line has four dashes to the inch, no other line should have more than two or fewer than eight dashes to the inch.

18. Using Lines to Connect Dots or Symbols

If lines connect visible dots or other symbols, make these dots or symbols at least twice as thick as the line, as shown in Figure 12.12 (Mr. Magoo).

19. Drawing Lines That Connect Different Symbols

If lines connect different symbols, use symbols that are easy to tell apart for points connected by different lines—such as those shown in Figure 12.13 (Mr. Magoo).

EXAMPLE: Plus signs, open circles, filled triangles, and filled circles remain distinct even when reduced to small sizes. However, the difference between filled and unfilled versions of the same element (such as • versus o) may be difficult to discern when the graph is projected at a small size.

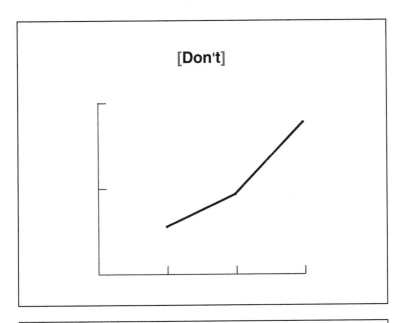

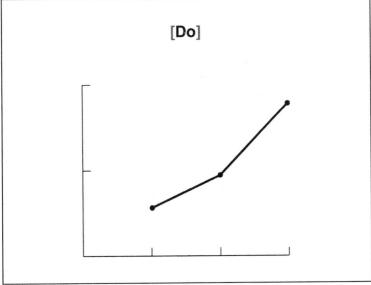

FIG 12.12

The points on the lines are especially important and should be emphasized by dots that are easy to distinguish from the line.

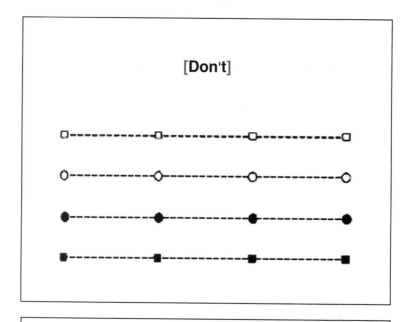

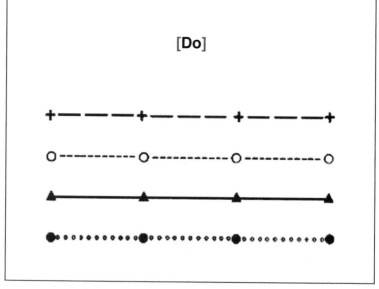

FIG 12.13

Studies have shown that the four lines and symbols on the bottom are very easy to distinguish.

20. Illustrating Approximate Relative Percentages

Use a pie graph to illustrate how a whole is divided into separate components (Judging the Book by Its Cover).

21. Conveying Precise Values

As a general rule, do not use a pie graph to illustrate precise amounts, such as the percentage of one part. However, this is not a problem if the amount of interest is 25%, 50%, or 75%, which is easy to discern at a glance (Mr. Magoo).

If you need to convey precise amounts while still depicting relative proportions with pie graphs, label the wedges—either by putting the numbers in them (if space permits) or next to them (Birds of a Feather). Do not provide a scale (Figure 12.14).

> EXAMPLE: It is easy to use the "Do" graph in Figure 12.14 to get a general sense of the relative proportions, but difficult to use the "Don't" graph to determine that there were 13% more car and mobile home loans than bank and finance loans.

22. Using Exploded Pies

Explode a segment or segments to emphasize them, as in "Do" in Figure 12.15. But do not explode more than one quarter of the wedges. If too many wedges are exploded, as they are in "Don't," the audience members won't know where to look. I offer 25% as a rough guideline, although there is no hard and fast percentage: The critical consideration is that enough wedges remain in the pie to make the exploded wedges disrupt the contour of the whole (Rudolph the Red-Nosed Reindeer).

23. Arranging Wedges

Unless there are reasons to order the wedges in a specific way, it will be easiest to compare the wedges if they are arranged in order of size (Birds of a Feather). In general, order from smaller to larger, with size increasing clockwise (Figure 12.16). Because values on a clock face increase in a clockwise direction, we expect greater quantities to be indicated by greater arcs in a clockwise direction (Judging the Book by Its Cover).

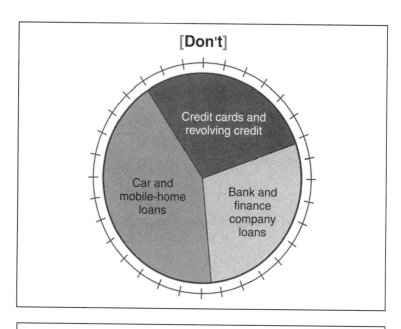

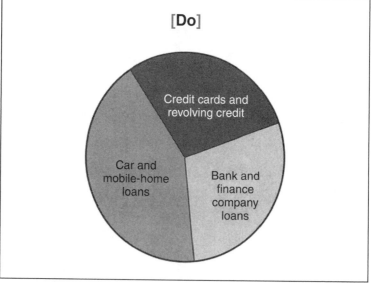

FIG 12.14

Do not use a scale with pie graphs; the viewer will have to struggle to count the number of ticks. In this graph, credit cards and revolving credit are the topic of interest, and hence this information is most visually immediate.

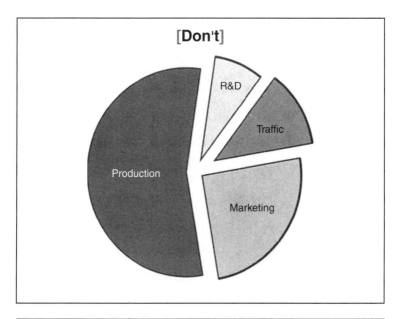

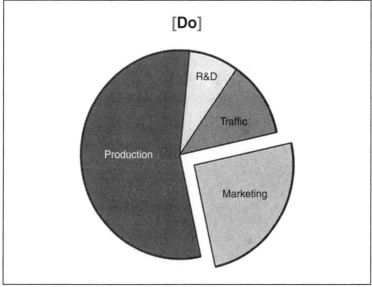

FIG 12.15
If too many wedges are exploded, none stands out.

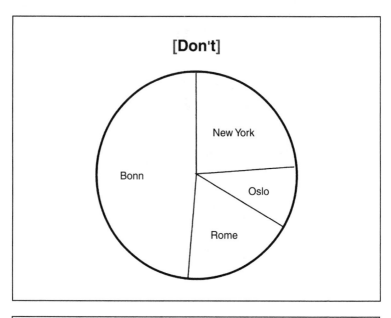

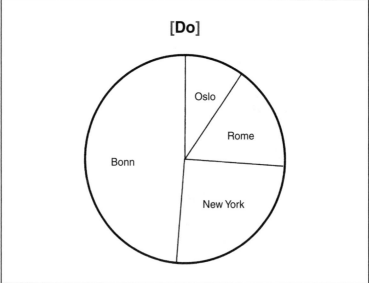

FIG 12.16

In Western culture, viewers expect quantities to increase clockwise around a circle.

However, if you wish to emphasize the larger components, put the largest at the top or in the "1 o'clock" position (the first that the viewer will focus upon when scanning in a clockwise order), and arrange the other wedges in decreasing size from this anchor point (Judging the Book by Its Cover).

24. Using Multiple Pies

If proportions vary greatly, don't use multiple pies to compare corresponding parts (Birds of a Feather). Instead, if the proportions are very different and the audience members are supposed to compare specific components, use a bar graph.

EXAMPLE: Compare the two pies in the "Don't" version of Figure 12.17. The relevant wedges are in different locations in the two pies—a shift that cannot be avoided when the proportions vary widely in the two pies. In contrast, in "Do" it is easy to compare multiple pies when the wedges are in roughly the same positions in each, and hence are easy to group.

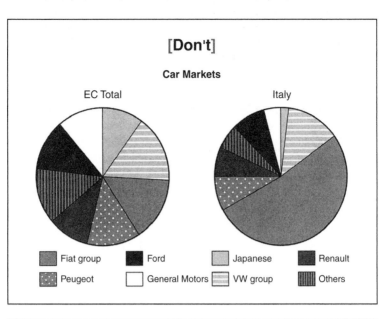

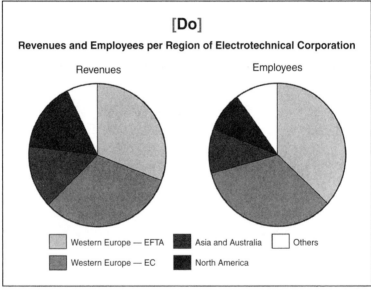

FIG 12.17

Corresponding wedges are hard to compare if, as in "Car Markets," they are not in corresponding positions.

Epilogue: Letting Science Have the Last Word

You might wonder whether the many recommendations I've made are just common sense; when you see them written out and stop to think about them, many of them probably appear to be. But if they are common sense, people should know them without being taught, and so should be able to apply them—even if the rules and recommendations have not been explicitly spelled out, as I've done here.

To find out whether the recommendations are common sense, my colleagues and I conducted another study (in addition to the one I described in Chapter 1): We took "Do/Don't" pairs of illustrations that are shown in *Clear and to the Point* (some of which are also used here) and removed the "Do/Don't" labels. We then randomly put one panel on the left and one on the right, so that half had the "Do" example on the left and the "Don't" example on the right and vice versa for the other half. We also created a second set of these pairs, reversing the positions (in order to remove the influence of any preferences that people might have for things on the left versus the right). We produced additional pairs so that each of the Cognitive Communication Rules was adequately represented. We then showed the pairs to Harvard students and to members of the local community (half receiving each version of the pairs, so that each panel appeared equally often on the left or right) and asked them to select which version was better—and then to explain their decisions.

The results were straightforward. First, the list below contains the percentage of participants for each rule who selected at least one wrong member of the pair:

- Goldilocks: 96%
- Birds of a Feather: 98%
- Rule of Four: 96%
- Rudolph the Red-Nosed Reindeer: 98%
- Mr. Magoo: 90%
- Viva la Difference: 79%
- Judging the Book by Its Cover: 96%
- Pied Piper: 56%

Looked at another way, in the best case, only 44% of the participants were always correct—with examples of the Pied Piper rule.

We then asked whether the participants who made the correct choice actually understood why the "Do" example was better than the "Don't." Two researchers separately analyzed the explanations the participants gave for each choice (and were very similar in their evaluations). Given that these participants made the right choice, here are the percentages of people who failed to explain correctly why the "Do" was better than the "Don't" example, for at least one example of a rule:

- Goldilocks: 60%
- Birds of a Feather: 60%
- Rule of Four: 81%
- Rudolph the Red-Nosed Reindeer: 60%
- Mr. Magoo: 88%
- Viva la Difference: 58%
- Judging the Book by Its Cover: 67%
- Pied Piper: 62%

Without question, the rules are not as obvious as they might seem!

These findings are consistent with the results I described in Chapter 1, when we evaluated PowerPoint® presentations that had been posted on the web. Nevertheless, I was still surprised by how poorly those presentations fared when we evaluated them, and worried that we may have inadvertently inflated the number of violations. I was concerned that this may have occurred because, in order to get very high agreement between the evaluators, we adhered to the strict letter of the law: Each recommendation was interpreted as strictly as possible; for example, if the recommendation said "No more than two lines per bulleted entry," a presentation would be classified as having violated this recommendation if it had a single bullet point with two lines and one word on a third line. But it's questionable whether there's really much difference between two lines and two lines with a single additional word.

To address this concern, I asked two additional people to re-evaluate the presentations we downloaded from the web. I now asked them to classify a feature of a presentation as a violation only if they believed that it would actually impair communication. I also asked them to be liberal in making such evaluations—to err on the side of giving the designer the benefit of the doubt.

The results of this more liberal scoring again revealed widespread violations of the Cognitive Communication Rules. According to this scoring, the different rules were violated by the following percent of the presentations:

- Goldilocks: 77%
- Birds of a Feather: 36%
- Rule of Four: 100%
- Rudolph the Red-Nosed Reindeer: 72%
- Mr. Magoo: 98%
- Viva la Difference: 86%
- Judging the Book by Its Cover: 27%
- Pied Piper: 59%

Thus, our strict criterion did not seriously overinflate our measure of the number of barrels that contained bad apples.

We haven't done the next study yet, which is to give people this book, have them repair a few PowerPoint® presentations—and then test to see how well they can use the rules and recommendations. My bet is that after a bit of practice, the principles that underlie this approach will sink in, and people will improve dramatically. It should not be hard to learn new intuitions, to learn when a presentation will be effective without having to think through every bit explicitly.

Why am I making this bet? Because we humans remember individual instances and automatically apply these remembered instances to new cases. So, as you see more examples of good versus bad ways to make and use slideshows, and understand why they are good or bad, you will store this information in your memory—which has the positive side effect of also training your intuition so that you can use this information in the future. Furthermore, we all should be able to learn these rules and recommendations easily: These guidelines are rooted in facts about the human mind, which we will find natural because we are accustomed to the ways of humans.

With all due respect to Mr. Aitken, whose words opened Chapter 1, it's now time for a change. Repeat after me: "I am a PowerPoint® Jedi; I use my skills at PowerPoint® to make difficult concepts comprehensible, memorable, and compelling. Embrace the bright side."

Index

Note: An "*f*" following a page number indicates figures.